Bridging the Gap: Achieving Efficiency in a Data-Hungry Wireless World

Vani

Contents

3   Methodology   53

4 Results and Discussion   67

Chapter 1

Introduction

1.1 Background

Generally each new generation of wireless communications attempts to improve the achievable data capacity of the radio access network in order to meet the forever changing user demands [1]. Cellular networks have particularly been undergoing growing data demands over the years [2]. From the early voice-centric first generation (1G) through to today's fourth generation (4G) wireless networks and beyond, each new generation was empowered with dramatic increases in data capacity compared to its predecessors.

Nevertheless device numbers and therefore data demands continue to soar as time goes by. Figure1.1 below shows mobile data demand forecast by CISCO [3]. According to [3], mobile data traffic grew 18 times over the five year period leading to 2016. As is forecast in Figure 1.1, the mobile data traffic is expected to grow exponentially to 49 exabytes per month in the year 2021. Given a forecast of such staggering data volumes, it is important to come up with technologies that have high spectral efficiency. Currently Long Term Evolution (LTE) Advanced, in an 8x8 Multiple Input Multiple Output (MIMO) configuration, can achieve up to 30 kbs/Hz as reported in [1].

In addition to high spectral efficiency requirement, energy efficiency is also a key requirement for the new access technologies to come [2]. Figure 1.2 shows the typical costs of deploying a network. As explained in [4], for both OPEX (Operational Expenditure) and CAPEX

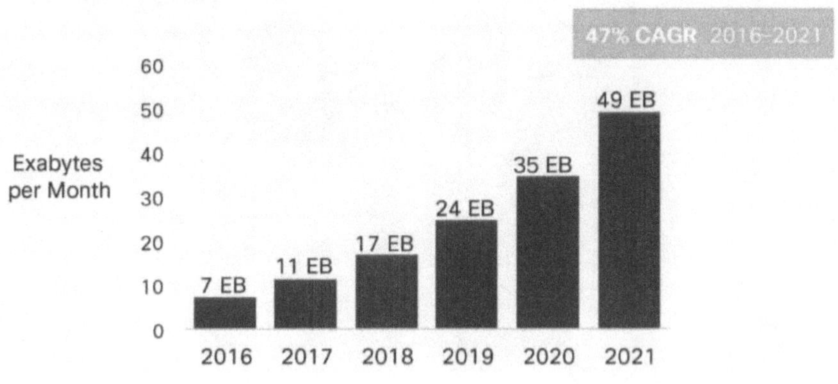

Figure 1.1: Mobile Data Demand Forecast [3]

(Capital Expenditure), the power consumed by the network costs more than 40% of the total cost of network deployment and running the network. With higher data demands in the future as predicted in [3], even more financial resources will be required to power the network, unless drastically more energy efficient methods are brought up. In [2], the authors explain that the demand in data services for LTE networks has seen energy consumption by LTE base stations increasing dramatically for most network operators. The authors go on to discuss various Energy Saving (ES) methods for LTE Networks.

Network operators generally employ at least one of three methods in order to cope with ever increasing data demands as explained in [4],[8]. The first way is densification of the network. This means operators have to acquire more sites to put up base stations in a given area. When more cells are added per unit geographical area, resources like frequency can be reused more frequently in order to accommodate more users. Baseband resources like 3G High-Speed Downlink Packet Access (HSDPA) channelization codes and Channel Elements (CE) available to users also get increased [8]. The signal to noise ratio (SNR) at the edge of the cell, which is normally the worst in the coverage area of the cell, increases with a denser network as the received signal strength is improved. Because of improved SNR, it becomes possible to employ higher order modulation techniques like 64 QAM (quadrature amplitude modulation) and thus improve the overall network capacity. This has seen operators deploying small cells

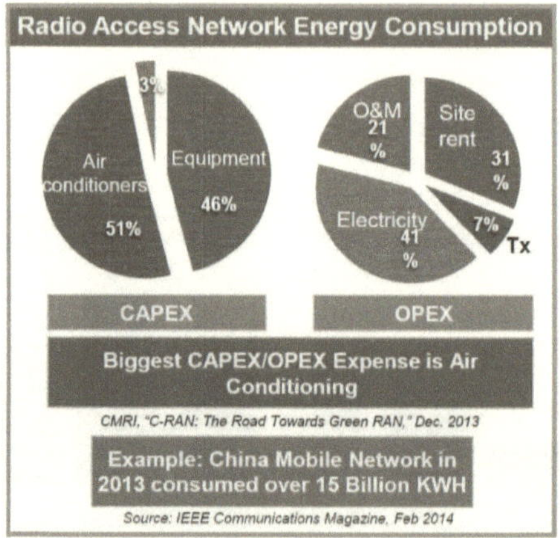

Figure 1.2: Radio Access Energy Consumption for Mobile Networks [4]

or even new macro cells in their networks. The overall result is higher achievable network capacity, though at a cost of more rentals, power costs and more equipment OPEX and CAPEX. The downside of increasing site capacity by adding more sites, in addition to the already stated costs, is the fact that interference in the network also generally increases, cutting on the gains made [4],[8].

Another way of increasing network capacity has been the further sectorization of the network [9],[10]. Instead of the traditional three sector sites, networks have had to split existing sectors up to as much as six sectors per given site. This necessitates employing more directional antennas which also tend to improve both coverage and capacity of a given network.

Some vendors like Commscope [9] and Huawei [10] have manufactured dual beam antennas with narrow beam widths, with 35 degree beam antennas being commonplace. These telecommunication equipment manufacturers have been manufacturing narrow dual beam antennas as part of their capacity improvement solution. The achievable data rates for each user will improve as does the power of the signal seen by each terminal. This is a consequence of Shannon's capacity equation given below, and explained in [8].

$$C = B \log_2(1 + SNR) \tag{1.1}$$

where C is capacity in bits/s, SNR is the Signal to noise ratio and B is the signal bandwidth. From equation (1.1), capacity is actually only proportional to the logarithm to base 2 of the SNR. Thus increasing the SNR is not such effective way of improving capacity. In [12], the author also explains that this method of capacity improvement inherently comes with its own problems. Power increment means interference seen by other users will also increase. This will force them to increase their power too. Most wireless networks are actually interference limited as explained in [13]. Thus densification is not exactly a panacea to solve network capacity issues.

As explained in [8], another method to increase the radio access capacity is to increase the bandwidth for each user. Capacity scales linearly with bandwidth according to Shannon's capacity equation. Bandwidth is thus a very effective way of improving capacity. 4G technologies like LTE, which uses up to 20 MHz, exploit that to improve capacity compared to predecessors like 3G which is standardized to use 5MHz. The inherent difficulty with this solution as explained in [14], is the scarcity of the spectrum in most parts of the world, particularly the spectrum below 6 GHz which is somewhat overcrowded. The authors in [14] go on to explain how adoption of the proposed Cognitive Radio (CR) technologies can help alleviate spectral shortages. In CR systems secondary users of the spectrum will opportunistically make use of the spectrum when and where the original primary users are not using it. In [15], researchers advocate for the use of mmWave spectrum in the coming generations of technology like 5G. This is in a bid to increase the capacity of the network by increasing bandwidth of the network. Although, increasing the bandwidth increases network capacity; it does not exactly address energy efficiency issues raised in [2].

The third method to increase capacity is increasing the number antennas for a given wireless access system as articulated in [4],[8],[12],[13],[16] and [17]. This brings about the realm of Multiple Input Multiple Output (MIMO) technologies. MIMO transmission systems are systems in which multiple antennas at the transmitter and receiver systems are used so as to provide independent and parallel streams of data and thus improve obtainable data rate [11]. Legacy MIMO means that multiple antennas will be configured at both the base station and the terminal. Up to 8 element antenna arrays have been defined in LTE [1],[18]. For LTE, with 8x8 MIMO configuration, peak spectral efficiency of 30 b/s/Hz can be achieved [1]. It is important to note that at the terminal, there are space and power constraints that make it difficult to implement many antennas. Out of necessity, a new form of MIMO called massive MIMO was thus borne. Massive MIMO uses many antennas, as many as multiple tens to perhaps hundreds of antennas at the base station to beamform the signal to single

(a) Legacy MIMO Antennas (Source : [41])

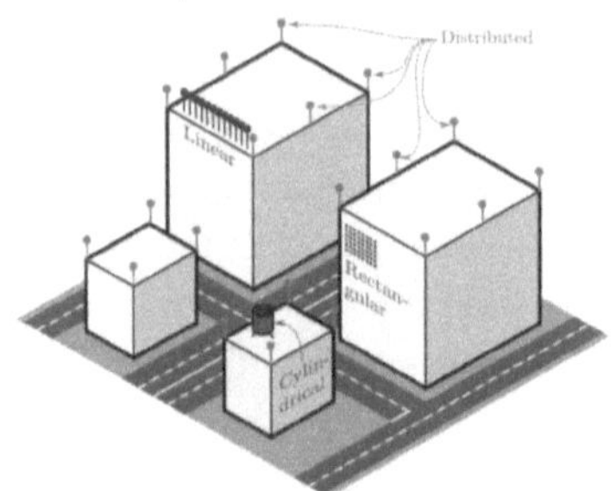

(b) Massive MIMO Antennas (Source : [41])

Figure 1.3: Legacy and possible massive MIMO antenna pictures

user terminals. Beamforming signals to specific users should improve the energy efficiency of the system as less energy will be radiated in a given cell. More antennas will provide more degrees of freedom for the propagation channel and thus exploit spatial multiplexing and provide higher data rates and more reliable links. Below 6 GHz, most wireless communication environments are dominated by Non Line of Sight (NLOS) [18]. This is because the receiver is often obstructed from the base station transmitter. Diffraction losses are low compared to higher frequencies. The coherence intervals are also longer. These conditions do favour the use of massive MIMO.

Figure 1.3 shows the comparison for legacy MIMO antennas and possible massive MIMO antennas. In Figure 1.3a the picture shows a typical three sectored base station with multiple antennas on each sector that propagates a single wide beam for its users. In Figure 1.3b several proposed massive MIMO antenna arrays are illustrated. These antenna arrays should be able to propagate multiple different beamformed signals to various users in a given sector.

In view of the given background on capacity and energy efficiency needs for wireless access systems, a lot of research has been underway to assess technologies that may potentially produce gains in capacity and consume reasonably less power [8]. Researchers have been touting massive MIMO as a potential candidate to achieve these. There is thus need to evaluate the potential of massive MIMO. This study will focus on massive MIMO, which is earmarked to be one of the effective technologies to realize 5G. The maximum achievable capacity of the MIMO channel, as is explained in [18], is given by:

$$C = \min(n_r, n_t) B \log_2(1 + SNR) \tag{1.2}$$

where n_t and n_r are number of transmitter and receiver antennas respectively.

1.1.1 The Massive MIMO Principle

As explained in [13], current systems like LTE send pilot waveforms to terminals in the downlink. The terminals use received pilots, which are known *a priori*, to calculate the effect of the wireless channel. The calculated channel responses form the channel state information (CSI) which the terminals then report to the base station (BS). These channel responses can then be used by the base station to precode downlink transmission data. In conventional MIMO, it would therefore mean that the BS would have to send as many pilots as there are antenna elements and the terminal would have to measure the associated channels and report back the CSI which would be difficult to realize practically. As explained in [13],[16],[17],[25],[26] in massive MIMO the BS will have up to hundreds of antennas so as to not only create multiple data streams but to also enable simplified signal processing owing to a process called channel hardening which averages out the randomness of the wireless channel. Massive MIMO is defined as a technology in which the base station is equipped with a very large number of antennas such that the spectral efficiency and energy efficiency are greatly improved as well as simplified linear signal processing made possible [17].

Knowing the location of a terminal is important in order for massive MIMO to be successful [4]. A simple way would be to transmit angular beams in multiple directions and let the terminal measure the direction with the strongest signal strength. Figure 1.4 shows 8 beams which can be sent to a user terminal. The direction from which the strongest response is received, which is assumed as the red beam in this case, locates the user terminal. The more the beams, the more accurate the method becomes. The data for the terminal can thus be steered into that direction using beamforming techniques. This method could work in a line of sight (LOS)environment. The majority of propagation channels below 6GHz, particularly in urban environments are NLOS [4].

This being the case, several studies including [13] - [25], have suggested using a time division duplex (TDD) based system to implement massive MIMO. This exploits the fact that the

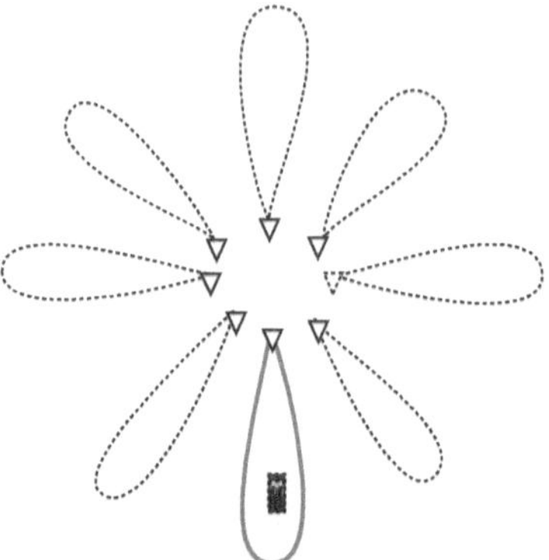

Figure 1.4: The Angular Beams Concept *Adapted from* [4]

uplink and downlink of a TDD based system are reciprocal. That means channel responses obtained in one direction are valid responses in the opposite direction [13]. The terminals send pilots to the BS, which will estimate the channel responses and assume their values for downlink channels. The BS will then precode the downlink data with these responses and be able to beamform the data to particular terminals. This method does work in most propagation environments. Figure 1.5 illustrates the massive MIMO concept.

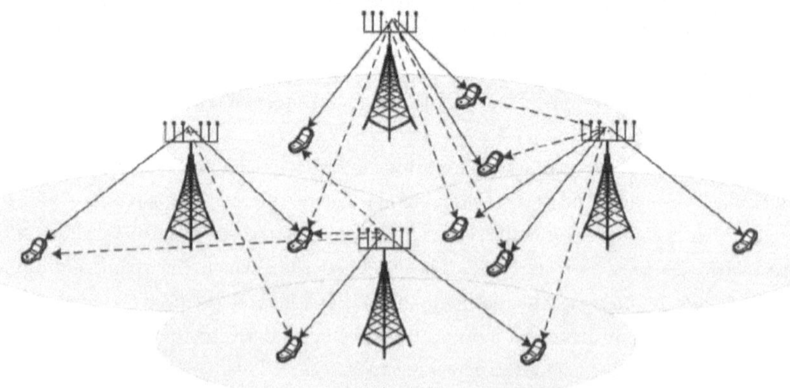

Figure 1.5: Massive MIMO Concept: [25]

Non-linear signal processing methods like dirty paper coding (DPC) and maximum likelihood (ML) may be used in massive MIMO [17] as they are optimal. They are however computationally more complex. As the number of antennas at the BS is increased, it is shown in [16] that linear signal processing methods can be used in massive MIMO. Maximal ratio combining (MRC), zero forcing (ZF), regularized zero forcing (RZF)and minimum mean square error (MMSE) are some of the methods that may be used [17]. For MRC, the received precoded signal is multiplied by the conjugate channel responses. ZF is a least squares approximation method which is used to approximate the transmitted signal from the received noisy signal. A linear set of equations which are more than the number of variables to be solved is formulated. RZF entails modifying the channel matrix by adding what is called a regularization factor that is used by ZF. This ensures that the regularised channel matrix has better properties. MMSE is also another linear method that estimates estimates the transmitted signal from the noisy received signal.

1.1.2   The Cost of Massive MIMO

In [18], the author explains that implementation of massive MIMO does involve certain costs, beyond those of the legacy MIMO approaches. Compared to legacy MIMO, masive MIMO introduces more radio frequency (RF) chains at the base station which support the beam forming antenna elements. The required signal processing is more complex and may require high power consumption. The physical space required to install multiple antennas at the base station also comes as a cost. As pointed out in [18], more energy will be consumed by the baseband processing. However it must be pointed out that the energy used to propagate beamformed data will be much less than legacy systems.

Table 1.1 shows the typical power consumption for a typical traditional macro base station. The base station typically consumes 3.45 kW. Of this, 0.65 kW is consumed by the base station equipment. Many operators have thousands of base stations. Finding energy efficient solutions that significantly cut down on consumed power would reduce their OPEX and increase profitability. Energy efficiency systems are also good for the environment.

Table 1.1: Typical Site Power Consumption [10]

Air Conditioner	Switching	Battery	Transmission	Total
0.65kW	0.2kW	0.2kW	0.2kW	3.45kW

In [27] the authors investigated the effect of MIMO on energy efficiency for LTE and LTE-A in macrocell and femtocell base stations. Their research showed that energy efficiency increases from SISO all the way through to 8x8 MIMO. It would thus be interesting to see what hundreds of massive MIMO does to energy efficiency of a base station.

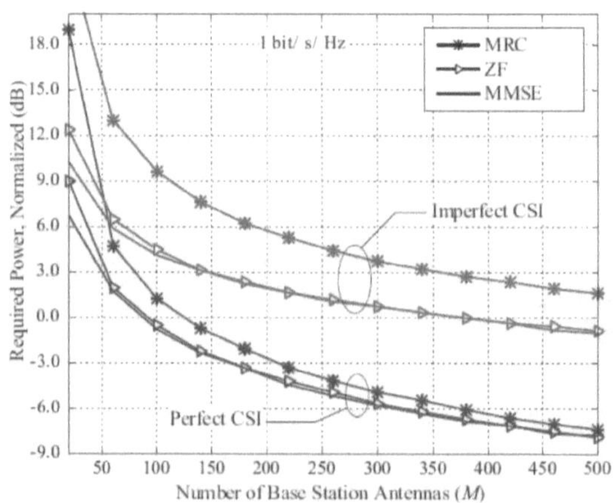

Figure 1.6: Normalized Power Consumption Per Antenna Element: [35]

Figure 1.6 shows the normalized power consumption as a function of the number of antenna elements for a massive MIMO system for MRC, ZF and MMSE receive combining methods. This simulation was done for systems that assume perfect channel state information (CSI) and one that assumes imperfect CSI. The result shows that the consumed power reduces as the number of antennas increase. Studies that confirm these trends are therefore very helpful to validate the energy efficiency gains of massive MIMO implementations.

Spectral efficiency is also an area that needs to be researched thoroughly for massive MIMO. Table 1.2 shows the uplink (UL) and downlink (DL) peak spectral efficiencies obtainable for 3rd Generation Partnership Project (3GPP)'s high speed packet access HSPA+ Release 8, LTE Release 8 and LTE Advanced standards. The peak spectral efficiency is obtained by dividing the peak data rate by the used bandwidth. Thus for 3GPP HSPA+ which uses 5Mhz and has peak down link speed of 21 Mbps, the peak spectral efficiency is 4.2 Mbps. The rest of the technologies are calculated the same way. LTE Advanced specifies up to 8x8 traditional MIMO configuration. This means that a user terminal has to have an 8 antenna element signal processing capability. This means more complex baseband processing and shorter battery life for a user terminal. The peak spectral efficiency for both LTE and LTE Advanced are shown in Table 1.2.

Table 1.2: Legacy Peak Spectral Efficiencies

Technology	Bandwidth [MHz]	Peak Data Rate	Peak Spectral Efficiency [b/s/Hz] DL/UL
HSPA+	5	21/11 Mbps	4.2/2.2
Rel. 8 LTE (4x4 MIMO)	20	300 Mbps/75 Mbps	15/3.75
LTE Advanced	20	1Gbps/1 Gbps	30/15

In comparison to the above spectral efficiencies, [13] and [28] did measurements and simulations
for the obtainable spectral efficiencies for massive MIMO using various linear signal processing
precoding/receive combining methods. Figure 1.7 shows that the spectral efficiency for
massive MIMO can reach up to nearly 13 b/s/Hz using Maximal Ratio Transmission for
precoding. This result is from measurements done using a linear array based massive MIMO
system in which there were 128 antenna elements and 4 single antenna user terminals. The
same setup with a cylindrical array obtained up to a spectral efficiency of up to more than 8
b/s/Hz. In Figure 1.8, the researchers did a simulation of massive MIMO spectral efficiency
as a function of the number of antenna elements for various receive combining methods. They
compared linear signal receive combining methods, namely zero forcing (ZF), regularized zero
forcing (RZF) and maximum ratio (MR) against minimum mean square error (MMSE). They
obtained up to 40 b/s/Hz spectral efficiency for linear signal receive combining methods.

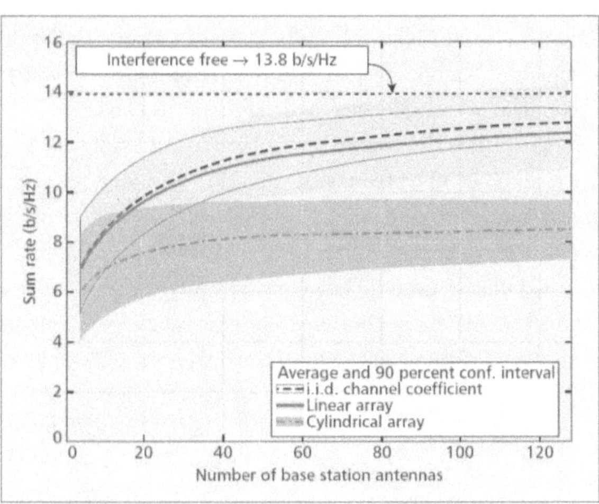

Figure 1.7: Spectral Efficiency for massive MIMO: [12]

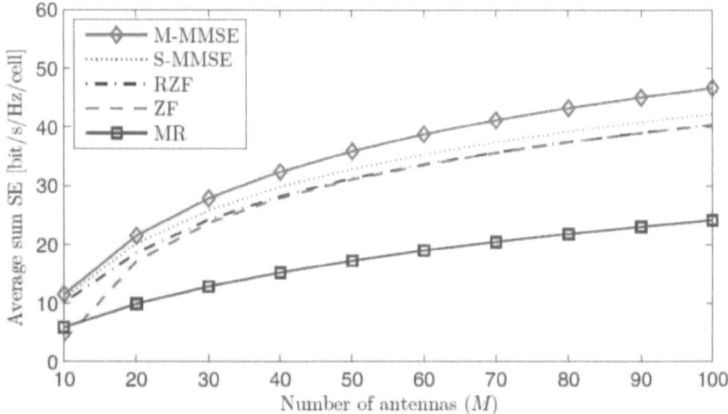

Figure 1.8: Spectral Efficiency for Massive MIMO: [28]

1.2   Motivation

Ever since massive MIMO was suggested in a seminal paper in [16], there has been a lot of research on the different aspects of massive MIMO. In [13] the authors point out that the motivation to study massive MIMO has been because of its potential to drastically improve the spectral efficiency and energy efficiency. Other advantages include possible reduction in latency, robustness against interference and jamming as explained in [13]. In [16], it is theoretically shown that the capacity of the massive MIMO Network grows without limit as a function of the number of antennas at the BS. The authors also explain that the channel inherently becomes deterministic as more antenna elements are added. The users get access to the whole time-frequency resources and thus removing any need for complex time or frequency scheduling of users. The potential benefits that may be brought about by implementation of massive MIMO are outlined in [15] through [25]. This technology is being touted as one of the potential game changing technologies for 5G wireless access systems.

In spite of all these potential benefits there is still a lot to be learnt about the feasibility of implementing massive MIMO. There are still plenty of research areas that need to be investigated. The research areas, as articulated in [13] include research on low cost hardware implementations, the effect of hardware imperfections, and baseband processing power consumption As explained in [8], there is definitely power to be saved by steering the electromagnetic radiation in the specific direction of the users as advocated for in massive MIMO, but there is also need to account for additional power owing to increased number of RF chains that must be implemented to build a massive MIMO system. There is also need to characterise the massive MIMO wireless channels as well as evaluating the effect of uplink/downlink reciprocity calibration methods. It is explained in [12], that the uplink and downlink are always reciprocal when evaluated within a channel's coherent time, but the associated RF hardware chains are not necessarily reciprocal. This necessitates the need to calibrate the downlink path against the uplink path when exploiting the obtained uplink channel responses in order to precode the downlink signal for beamforming. It is also explained that since pilot contamination may potentially have a big impact on the overall spectral and energy efficiency of massive MIMO systems, it is also necessary to study and evaluate different pilot reuse methods and their performance. Prototypes also need to be built in order to appreciate the potential benefits of massive MIMO. Several researches are still on going as far as these and other issues of this technology are concerned.

In [12],[13],[16],[17] and [18], it is explained that among the many research areas that need further research, fast and coherent signal processing methods that may be employed in massive MIMO realization need to be looked at. Linear precoding schemes and detection methods, need to be evaluated as they carry a huge amount of weight as far as determining whether massive MIMO will fulfill its potential as one of the enabling technologies for 5G and beyond technologies. This research is therefore intended to investigate the performance, and consequently the suitability, of linear signal processing methods that may be applied in massive MIMO. Some of the current research areas that need to be researched further are as listed below.

- Energy efficiency of massive MIMO Systems

- Spectral efficiency/capacity of massive MIMO Systems

- Development of appropriate channel models

- Prototype implementation - multiple RF chains, up/down convertors, analog to digital (A/D) and digital to analog (D/A) converters

- Research on reciprocity of uplink (UL) /downlink (DL) and possible calibration of UL base-lined against DL

- Pilot contamination and its effect on spectral and energy efficiency MIMO systems

- Performance of linear signal processing systems bench-marked against optimal non-linear signal processing systems.

- Deployment scenarios. This will consider backward compatibility with legacy systems.

- System studies and considerations for relationships with heterogeneous network solutions

1.3   Problem Statement

As was given by research area examples in section 1.2, among the plethora of new research areas in Massive MIMO is the signal processing required. It was stated in [16] that as the number of antennas approach infinity, the random statistics of the channel become more and more deterministic. The term "infinity" here, obviously, serves to highlight the scalability of the theoretical argument; in reality there would likely be a point at which additional antennas provides marginal benefit for a particular context; real systems would clearly have a finite number of antennas.

It is against such background, that as stated earlier, significant amount of research in various massive MIMO signal processing areas is needed. In [17] and [19] such non-linear methods like Dirty Paper Coding and Successive Interference Cancellation (SIC) may be used to detect massive MIMO signals. However as stated in [18], with an increased number of antennas, it becomes possible to use linear signal processing methods as they become near optimal with more antennas. Zero Forcing, Regularized Zero Forcing, Maximal Ratio Transmission and Wiener Filtering methods are some such signal processing methods that may be used. It is against this background that this study seeks to investigate the suitability of such signal processing methods under assumed realistic channel conditions. It is important to evaluate the massive MIMO performance for a given number of elements in the antenna array.

This work intends to build on the work already done by the research community and be able to evaluate the performance of massive MIMO in terms of such metrics as the spectral efficiency, in a wireless propagation environment.

There is a suitable number of antennas from which the wireless channel properties become deterministic enough that linear signal processing performance becomes near optimal. This number can be obtained through simulation of the obtainable spectral efficiency as a function of the number of antenna elements assumed for various sub-optimal receive combining methods. This performance can also be benchmarked against optimal but non-linear receive combining methods. Comparisons against spectral efficiencies prescribed for legacy systems like 3GPP's WCDMA and LTE can be done. Simulations can be done to determine if massive MIMO can offer spectral efficiencies recommended for 5G systems.

1.4 Research Objective

The objective of this research was to evaluate the performance of linear signal processing methods for massive MIMO in a wireless environment. This was done through analysing the obtainable spectral efficiency as a function of the number of antenna elements for some linear detection and precoding methods that may be implemented for massive MIMO systems. The other aspect was to investigate the effect of pilot contamination on the spectral efficiency performance for various linear signal processing methods. Linear signal processing methods like zero forcing, regularised zero forcing, maximal ratio combining and minimum mean square error detection and precoding methods were considered.

1.5 Research Questions

In order to evaluate the performance of linear signal processing methods for Massive MIMO, a number of research questions need to be answered.

- What would the spectral efficiency of massive MIMO be?

  - The answer to this question would be very important in determining whether massive MIMO can be adopted as one of the 5G enabling technologies. IMT-Advanced specifies a peak spectral efficiency of at least 15 b/s/Hz in the downlink direction. This is in addition to peak capacity of 1 Gbps in the downlink direction.

- What would be the optimum number of antennas per desired number of users in a massive MIMO system? The required computational complexity, the consumed power and the system complexity are the constraints to be considered.

- The answer to this question will help in accessing the practicality of implementing massive MIMO. Earlier studies indicate that the more antennas at the base station, the more deterministic the wireless channel becomes. It is however a fact that, the bigger the antenna arrays, the more space they will require. This will also possibly translate to more RF chains and more power consumption baseband processing. The optimum number of antennas is a trade-off between the spectral efficiency, power consumption, the system complexity and needed computational complexity.

- How would the spectral efficiency performance of the chosen linear signal processing methods like MMSE, ZF, RZF and MRC compare to one another?

  - Massive MIMO implementation will see large arrays deployed at the Base Station. Non-linear precoding and detection methods could be used because they are optimal. However they are so complex that it would be difficult to implement them in real systems. The answer to this research question will help determine whether linear precoding and detection methods which are sub-optimal can be used in place of the non-linear methods and achieve a similar spectral efficiency performance.

- What would be the effect of pilot contamination on the spectral efficiency of massive MIMO systems?

  - Pilot contamination is a reality in massive MIMO when the pilot reuse factor exceeds 1. It was considered important to investigate the effect of the pilot reuse factor adopted and establish if an optimum value that maximizes the spectral efficiency of a massive MIMO network can be obtained given the reality of a finite number of pilot sequences in a mobile network.

1.6 Project Scope and Limitations

This study was done using simulations in MATLAB. Important insights into massive MIMO were drawn from the analysis of simulated results for different linear signal processing methods and assumed antenna array sizes. There was no access to measurement equipment for more realistic wireless channels and therefore the scope of this study was limited to simulations.

In [28], the author assumed up to 100 elements and 10 users in a cell. In this study, antenna array sizes of up to 200 elements were looked at. Arrays which are more than 200 elements place demand more computing resources and could not be achieved on an ordinary laptop. The number of antenna elements assumed was always greater or equal to the assumed number of users in a given cell. The assumption is that the admission control policy will not admit users whose number is greater than a given number of antenna elements in a cell. Monte Carlo simulations were done to determine the spectral efficiency for randomly generated user locations within a given cell. Receive combining methods and precoding methods that were used were namely; zero forcing (ZF), regularised zero Forcing (RZF), maximal ratio combining (MRC) and minimum mean square error (MMSE) methods.

The idea was to compare spectral efficiency as a function of the assumed number of antenna elements for linear receive combining methods and precoding methods. The assumed system was initially be restricted to a single cell. This meant that pilot contamination was not considered for this particular scenario. A cell area of one square km was considered. The signal angular spread about a given nominal angle at the receiver was assumed to be normally distributed, with the angular standard deviation (ASD) of up to 10 degrees. This agrees with the suggestion that in urban environments the ASD should be less than 15 degrees [22]. A second scenario which assumed 16 square cells was assumed. Lastly a 64 square cell grid network was also modeled. In these two scenarios the effect of pilot contamination was analyzed. Pilot reuse factors of 1, 2, 4 and 8 were analysed.

Square cells were assumed in the network model used. In real propagation environment, cells are of no such regular shape. This model was used to simplify analysis.

Table 1.3: Simulation Parameters

Parameter	Value
Number of BS or Cells	1,16,64
Number of UEs, K	20,3
Number of Antennas, M	20:200
Number of Simulations runs	100
Samples per coherence block, (τ_c)	200
UL transmit Power	20 dBm
Pathloss Exponent, (α)	3.76
Channel gain at 1km	-148.1dB
Shadow fading Standard Dev, σ_{sf}	10
Cell Area	1km x 1km
Pilot Reuse factors	1, 2, 4 and 8

For channel estimation, the MMSE estimation method inherited from [28] is to be used to estimate the wireless channel. This means the effects of pilot contamination brought about in a multi-cellular environment was not be observable.

In order to investigate the effect of pilot contamination, a 16 cell grid and 64 cell grid networks were also studied. This was done for both precoding and receive combining signal processing methods.

1.7 Research Contributions

The findings of this research were presented at an IEEE International Conference on Information Management and Industrial Engineering to be held in Cape Town [52]. The authors presented the simulation results that were obtained for SE trends for the linear detection methods for a single cell and a 16 cell grid networks.

1.8 Document Outline

This section describes the structure of this book. It briefly summarizes each of the chapters of this book.

Chapter 1 introduces the background behind the massive MIMO research field. The section discusses the massive MIMO principle and also seeks to point to the existing research gaps as guided by the literature. The motivation for this research and the problem statement of this research are discussed. This then led to the definition of the research objectives, the research questions and lastly the project scope and limitations.

Chapter 2 provides an in-depth review of the current research works in the massive MIMO field. Various linear signal processing methods that can be applied to massive MIMO implementation were discussed. Linear signal processing methods were known to be sub-optimal compared to the non-linear methods like Dirty Paper Coding. The performance of the linear signal processing methods need to be investigated under massive MIMO regime. This chapter laid some background to the construction of a massive MIMO system which combine beamforming, phased array antenna and MIMO concepts. The foundation of this work was built from works already have already done as was cited in various literature.

Chapter 3 presents the simulation environment that was designed and built in MATLAB in order to analyze massive MIMO performance in the assumed propagation environment. Simulations for the performance of linear signal processing receive and precoding methods were done. Obtainable spectral efficiency was evaluated for varying number of antenna to users ratio in a correlated channel and an uncorrelated channel. Three simulation network models were designed. The first one was a single cell network with one base station and 20 users. The second and third models had 16 and 64 cell grid networks respectively. A general increase in the spectral efficiency was expected as the assumed array sizes were increased. The relative performance of the linear signal processing methods was evaluated. The importance of increasing the number of antennas could therefore be observed. In addition, the spectral efficiency performance of various signal processing methods were also evaluated against angular spread observed at the users. The effect of the size of the pilot reuse factor was also to be evaluated.

Chapter 4 presents results from the simulation of a massive MIMO system in MATLAB. The results obtained were divided into three sections. The first section looked at spectral efficiency trends as a function of the number of antennas assumed at a massive MIMO base station. A single cell was assumed. This was done for MMSE, ZF, RZF and MR linear receive combining and precoding methods. These simulations were initially done for an ideally uncorrelated wireless channel, which imply orthogonal streams of data to users. It was then decided to introduce some level of correlation to the wireless channel and do the same Spectral Efficiency simulations. The second section looked at spectral efficiency as a function of the Angular Standard Deviation (ASD) about the nominal angle at the receiver. The distribution of the ASD is assumed to be normally distributed about its nominal value. The second section looked at the spectral efficiency trends obtainable using a 16 cell model. The last section looked at results obtained using a 64 cell model. The effect of the pilot reuse fact was more fully observed.

Chapter 5 analyzes and discusses the results of the simulations done. The chapter compares the spectral efficiency performance for MMSE, ZF, RZF and MR against each other. The trends obtained for the performance of these receive combining and precoding methods as a function of the Angular Standard Deviation of the signal about its nominal value at the receiver as observed in Chapter 4 was also discussed. The results obtained for the 16 cell and

64 cell network model based simulations were also discussed. This chapter also discusses the limitations of the conclusions that could be derived from the experiments done in Chapter 4.

Chapter 6 presents the conclusions drawn from this research as a whole. The chapter re-looks at the initial research objectives and to what extent they were achieved. The chapter explicitly states the obtained spectral efficiency values for a massive MIMO system and the corresponding number of antennas that will make the linear signal processing methods like MMSE, Zero Forcing and Maximal Ratio Combining achieve the observed spectral efficiency values. Some insights that were obtained from this study are drawn out.

Lastly future works and recommendations were proposed in Chapter 7. The chapter concludes by recommending more simulations using such planning tools as Atoll with digital maps that will obtain more insights into issues that may arise from deploying a massive MIMO system.

Chapter 2

Literature Review

2.1 Introduction

This Chapter seeks to lay a theoretical foundation for the various aspects that pertain to the realization of massive MIMO systems. It also reviews the metrics and terminology used in this study. It references to the concepts and study results from various sources in published literature works. Massive MIMO can conceptually be understood as a combination of the MIMO concept and beam-forming concept. Using this approach, the concepts behind MIMO are first discussed. Some of the concepts require understanding of linear algebra. Of particular importance is the MIMO channel matrix singular value decomposition method. After looking at MIMO, the beamforming concept is studied. Beamforming requires understanding such concepts as digital beam-forming and analog beamforming. The use of phased array systems in order to perform beamforming was also discussed. With these component technologies that may conceptually be seen as constituting massive MIMO having been discussed, the last part of this chapter then looks at the massive MIMO concept as a whole. The propagation effects on massive MIMO wireless channel were also analyzed. Signal processing methods that may be applied to massive MIMO channels are then analyzed. These signal processing methods are divided into precoding and detection signal processing methods. The chapter ends by pointing to the necessary investigations in performance of linear detection methods, which the next chapter will develop methodologies to do so.

The layout of this chapter is as given in Fig.2.1.

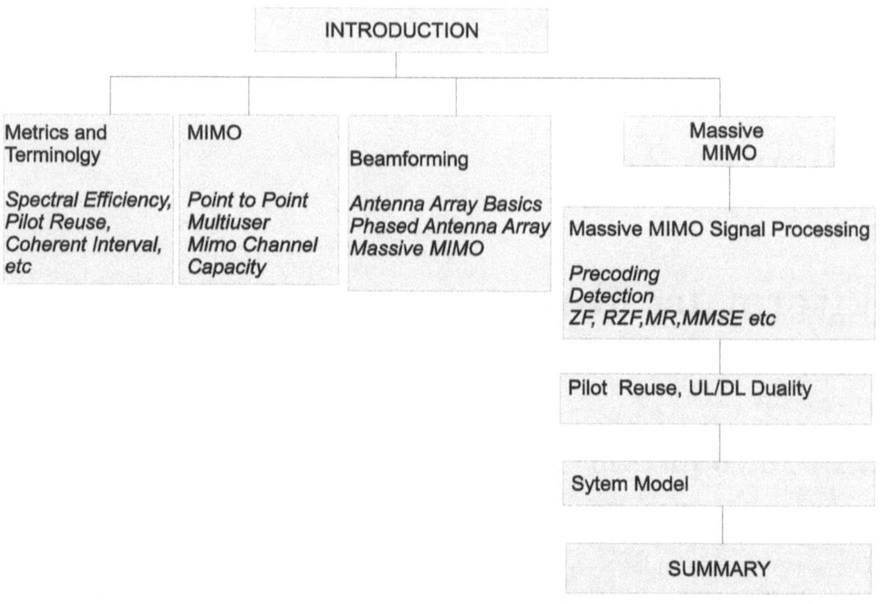

Figure 2.1: Literature Review layout

2.2   Metrics and Terminology

Some of the main metrics and terminology used in this **book** are as follows :

- Spectral efficiency - this is defined in [20] as the amount of data bandwidth that can be obtained from a given technology per unit frequency spectrum used. It is measured in bits per second per Hz (bps/Hz). From equation (1.1), the spectral efficiency (SE) is given by :

$$SE = \log_2(1 + SNR) \tag{2.1}$$

were SNR is the signal to noise ratio.

- M - The number of antenna elements installed at a Massive MIMO base station

- Pilot reuse factor f - defined in [21], [22] as is the rate at which pilot resources may be reused in the network.

- Coherent Interval - defined in [23] as the interval in which the channel maybe considered static. It is made up of the coherent bandwidth, B_c and the coherent time T_c. It is measured in the number of complex samples.

- UE - the user terminal in a cellular systems. The number of UEs is a cell was denoted K

The metrics above were selected for explanation in this subsection as they shall be used most frequently throughout the text. The rest shall be explained when they are used.

2.3 Multiple Input Multiple Output (MIMO)

Multiple Input Multiple Output (MIMO) improves the data capacity of a network through spatial multiplexing or the overall performance through diversity. With diversity such metrics as the Bit Error Rate (BER) will improve as the Signal to Noise Ratio (SNR) is improved. To obtain multiplexing gain, the MIMO system uses knowledge of the channel gain matrix to create independent parallel data streams. High Spectral efficiencies are thus obtained using MIMO. This comes at the cost of more space to install the antennas, more power for baseband processing and more complex multidimensional signal processing. The use of multiple antennas at the transmitter or receiver brings about diversity. Diversity helps to mitigate the effects of multipath fading by primarily establishing independent paths for the wireless signal. There are a number of ways of providing diversity [17]. The first way is polarization diversity. Two antennas with horizontal and vertical polarization are used to transmit and or receive signals. The scattering angles for the two signals are random and therefore likely to cause the signal to fade at different times. Two disadvantages for this method of creating independent paths exist. The first one is the fact that only two independent fading paths can be created. The second one is that the transmitted power has to be halved, implying a 3dB loss in power. The second way of creating independent diversity paths is called time diversity. In this method the same signal is transmitted a multiple of time with a separation of at least the channel coherence time. The disadvantage with this method is that it reduces the obtainable data rates since the same signal has to be transmitted at least twice. The third way of creating path diversity is through frequency diversity. Frequency diversity means the signal is transmitted at different carrier frequencies which separated by the coherence bandwidth of the channel. The fourth and final way to create path diversity to be discussed in this **book** is called space diversity. Multiple antennas at the transmitter and receiver can be used so as to coherently combine multiple copies of the signal such that a signal with high signal to noise ratio is obtained. This brings about what is called array gain. By appropriately weighting signals sent to antenna elements at the transmitter, diversity gain is obtained. Diversity gain refers to the gradient error probability curve that result from diversity combining. This **book** focuses more on space diversity.

2.3.1 Point to Point MIMO

For Point to Point Single User MIMO (SU-MIMO) as explained in [7], a single multiple antenna transmitter communicates with another single multiple antenna receiver. This is pictorially show in Figure 2.2. This MIMO version is not practically scalable as the user terminal is ordinarily of limited processing power and is relatively small in size. In this mode, high data rates for a single user can be obtained. This is because of array gain and diversity gain obtained with the advent of MIMO.

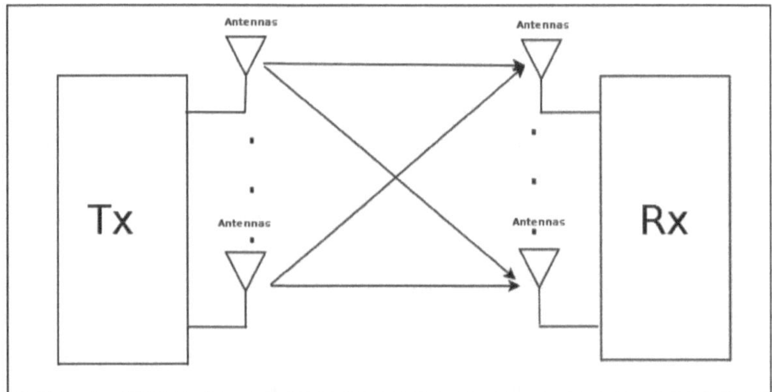

Figure 2.2: Single-User MIMO

2.3.2   Multi-User MIMO

Figure 2.3 shows Multi-User MIMO (MU-MIMO) system. A set of spatially separated users with one or more antennas communicates with a base station with multiple antennas. The system exploits extra spatial degrees of freedom. The base station precodes user data using the channel matrix information. MU-MIMO exploits multiplexing gain. Multiplexing gain is obtained from the fact that independent data streams can be transmitted through independent fading paths formed through the use of multiple antennas in a MIMO system.

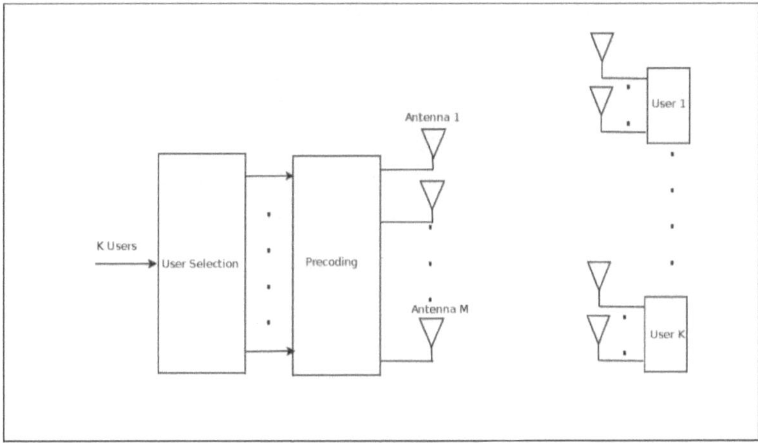

Figure 2.3: Multi-User MIMO

2.3.3   Parallel Decomposition of the MIMO channel

The analysis of the MIMO channel through singular value decomposition (SVD) of the MIMO channel matrix is explained in [17]. The received signal is given by the equation below

$$y = Hx + n \tag{2.2}$$

where $\mathbf{x}$ is the transmitted vector of signals and $\mathbf{n}$ is the noise. The transmitted signals $\mathbf{x}$ is also given by :

$$x = T\tilde{x} \tag{2.3}$$

where $\mathbf{x}$ refers to transmitted symbols and $\mathbf{T}$ is the precoding matrix which multiplies symbols so as to maximize some desired performance measure. $\mathbf{T}$ is designed to achieve zero interference between users. i.e

$$[\mathbf{HT}]_{j,k} = 0 \text{ for } k \neq j$$

This is equivalent to :

$$\mathbf{HT} = \text{diag}\sqrt{\mathbf{p}}$$

where $\sqrt{\mathbf{p}} = [\sqrt{p_1}...\sqrt{p_K}]$ and p_K is the transmitted power for each independent MIMO path.

The received signal is given by the equation 2.3. The MIMO channel can be decomposed into R_H parallel independent channels. If we assume a channel matrix $\mathbf{H}$ with rank R_H we can perform a singular value decomposition (SVD) to the channel matrix in order to decompose the channel into independent channels.

$$\mathbf{H} = \mathbf{U}\mathbf{\Lambda}\mathbf{T}^H \tag{2.4}$$

where $\mathbf{U}$ is an M_r by M_r **unitary** matrix and $\mathbf{T}$ is an $M_t \mathrm{x} M_t$ unitary matrix. A **unitary** matrix means $\mathbf{U}^H\mathbf{U} = \mathbf{I}_{M_t}$ and $\mathbf{T}^H\mathbf{T} = \mathbf{I}_{M_t}$. $\mathbf{\Lambda}$ is a diagonal matrix of the singular values of matrix $\mathbf{H}$. The singular values of $\mathbf{H}$ are given by : $\sigma_i = \sqrt{\lambda_i}$ where λ_i is the ith eigenvalue of $\mathbf{HH}^H$ and R_H is the rank of the matrix. M_t and M_r are the number of transmit antennas and receive antennas respectively.

$$R_H \leq \min\left(M_t, M_r\right) \tag{2.5}$$

The decomposition of the MIMO channel can be done at the transmitter through *precoding* and at the receiver through *receiver shaping*. The diagram in Figure 2.4 shows the MIMO channel decomposed into parallel channels with gain σ_i where $i = 1, ..., R_H$. The values of the obtained gains σ_i can be used to optimally distribute power to the channels so as to maximize the capacity of the MIMO channel.

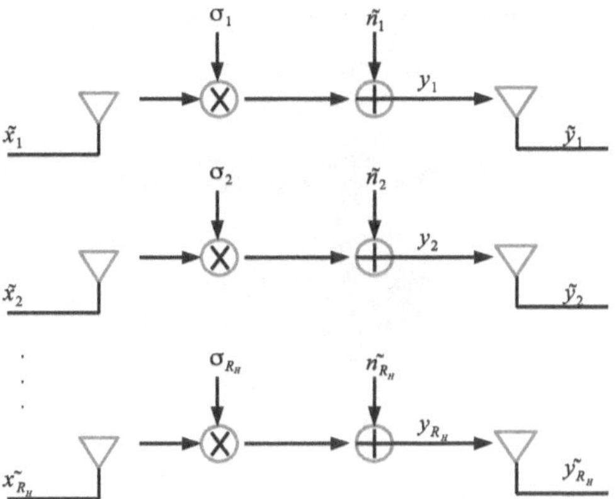

Figure 2.4: MIMO Channel decomposition: [17]

2.3.4 MIMO Channel Capacity

The capacity of a MIMO channel depends on the obtained channel gains and the knowledge of the channel matrix at either the receiver or transmitter.

Waterfilling

The capacity of a MIMO channel depends on where and how much of the channel matrix is known. If the channel matrix is known at the transmitter a power allocation algorithm called waterfilling may be used. The method seeks to optimize the overall capacity of a given channel by allocating the most power resources to the sub-channels with the best gains. In [17], the capacity of the MIMO channel for a rank R_H channel matrix is derived to be as below:

$$C = \max_{\rho:\sum_i \rho_i \leq P} \sum_{i=1}^{R_H} B \log_2(1 + \sigma_i^2 \rho_i) \tag{2.6}$$

The channel can thus be decomposed into R_H channels and is said to have R_H degrees of freedom. Here $\rho = \frac{P}{\sigma^2}$. The capacity can therefore be given by:

$$C = \max_{\rho:\sum_i \rho_i \leq P} \sum_{i=1}^{R_H} B \log_2(1 + \frac{\sigma_i^2 \rho_i}{\sigma^2}) \tag{2.7}$$

$$= \max_{\rho:\sum_i \rho_i \leq P} \sum_{i=1}^{R_H} B \log_2(1 + \frac{P_i \gamma_i}{P}) \tag{2.8}$$

where $\gamma_i = \frac{\sigma_i^2 P}{\sigma^2}$ is the SNR associated with the ith channel.

2.4   Beamforming

Conceptually, beamforming may be thought of as the ability of a radio transmitter to direct relatively narrow signals to intended receivers. However in actual fact, beamforming refers to the preconditioning of the signals at the transmitter by matching the given wireless channel conditions so that the signals will add constructively at the desired receiver and destructively elsewhere. Beamforming comes in two main variants: digital beam forming and analog beamforming [1]. The analog and digital beamforming concepts are shown in Figure .

For massive MIMO, digital beamforming is of more interest. This is because communication below 6GHz is predominantly NLOS. Analog beamforming entails using an antenna array to direct the beam in one particular environment at a time. Digital beamforming is so flexible that in NLOS environment, the precoding of the signal is such that the various signal components will reinforce each other at the desired terminal location and destructively interfere at other terminal locations.

User Terminal Location

Getting to know the user terminal location is indeed invaluable. One approach would be to use angular beams and then beamform data to the direction with the strongest signal.

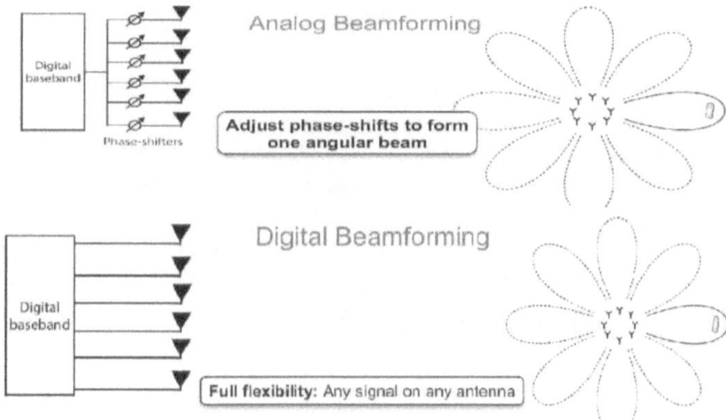

Figure 2.5: Beamforming theory : [4]

This works in LOS environments only. For massive MIMO the user sends pilot signals to the base station which will use these to estimate the channel. This will work in a TDD scenario where the downlink and uplink use the same frequency.

2.4.1 Antenna Array Basics

Figure 2.6 shows a typical phased antenna array as well as the resultant directed beam. All the antennas are fed with the same signal but each with a different phase [50],[49]. The different phases are used to influence the overall radiation pattern formed by all the antennas. The power of all the elements is the same but their phases are controlled by the phase shifter that is attached to each antenna. This results in a directed beam as shown.

In order to understand how the phase determines the direction of the antenna array, the diagram in Figure shows a basic two element phased array. Two adjacent antennas separated by a distance d, as shown in the diagram, result in electromagnetic signals whose path difference x is given by:

$$x = dsin\theta \tag{2.9}$$

The phase difference between the two signals, ϕ, can be obtained from :

$$\frac{\phi}{2\pi} = \frac{dsin\theta}{\lambda}$$

(2.10)

where λ is the wavelength of the signals and θ is the direction (steering angle) of the signals. Clearly by controlling ϕ we can control θ. This is because the phase difference between the signals will determine where they reinforce each other and where they cancel each other (constructive and destructive interference). This theory forms the basis for beamforming.

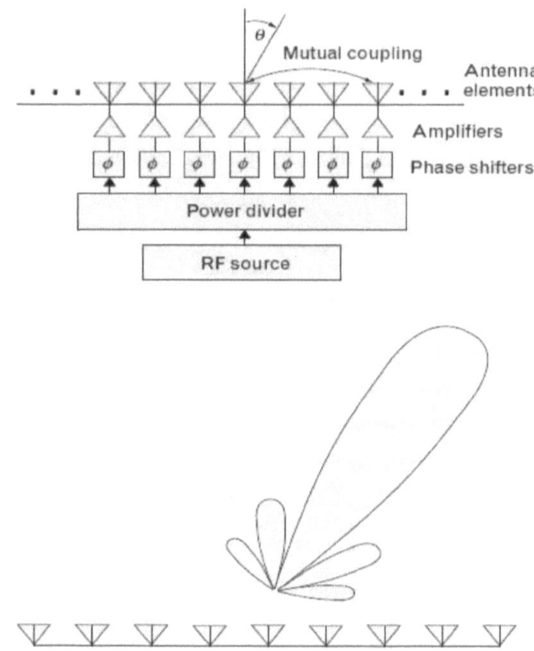

Figure 2.6: Antenna array theory: [49]

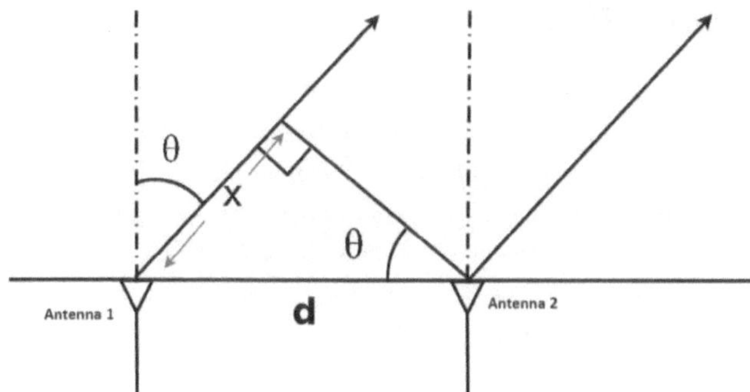

Figure 2.7: Antenna Array Basics

2.4.2 Phased Array based Massive MIMO Systems

Phased array systems are very useful in the implementation of massive MIMO [6]. The signal to each antenna is weighted by uplink measured complex channel responses which confer beamforming directivity to the signals meant for each user terminal. The weights used in [4] (w_1, w_2, w_3) are the complex channel realizations, h_{11}, h_{12}, h_{13}. These will direct the signals such that they will reinforce each other at the desired user location and cancel each other elsewhere. The effect is such that the signals will be beamformed to users as shown in Figure 2.8.

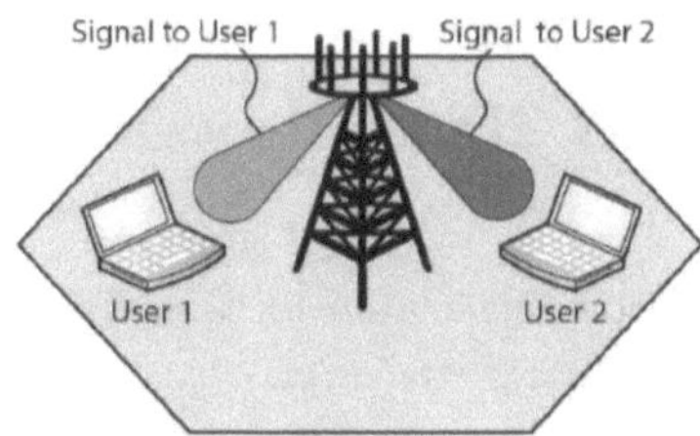

Figure 2.8: Multi-antenna transmission: [4]

2.5 Massive MIMO

The evolution of multi-user MIMO has seen the birth of massive MIMO. Massive MIMO can be seen as the combination of MIMO and beamforming [16]. It is also important to understand phased array antenna basics in order to understand massive MIMO. This chapter looks at the Massive MIMO concepts, beamforming and phased array antenna concepts. There are still ongoing research works that seek to understand the potential of massive MIMO as one of the 5G enabling technologies [16].

2.5.1 Massive MIMO Channel Capacity

As the BS antennas are increased a Massive MIMO systems is obtained. It is shown in [18] that the capacity of a massive MIMO system is given by

$$C = \max \sum_{k=1}^{K} \log_2(1 + M\rho\beta) \tag{2.11}$$

where M, ρ and β represent the number of BS antennas, the signal to noise ratio and the large scale fading coefficients respectively. K represents the number of user terminals and is typically much less than M. Figure 1.5 shows a typical massive MIMO system. The base station has multiple antennas while the user terminals have single antenna devices. The number of terminals is typically less than the number of antennas.

2.6 Massive MIMO Signal Processing

Signal processing techniques applicable in a wireless communication system may broadly be categorized into linear and non-linear precoding and detection methods. Non-linear methods are optimal but they require more computational resources compared to linear methods which are generally sub-optimal. This work seeks to study the performance of non-linear signal processing methods applicable to massive MIMO. If the channel matrix is known at the transmitter, then precoding is applicable. If the channel is known at the receiver, then detection or receive combining is applicable.

In massive MIMO, the BS has as many as hundreds of antennas. When the number of antenna elements increases, several consequences occur as explained in [13],[16],[17]. The random statistics of the channel converge to become more deterministic leading to the disappearance of small scale fading effects. Small scale fading refers to the degradation of the wireless channel owing to constructive and destructive interference of various multipath components of a signal which take different paths from the transmitter to the receiver and thereby arrive with different delays and amplitudes.

The channel becoming more deterministic brings about what is called *channel hardening* [12],[13]. This means that though the effective channel gain is still random its statistical expectation can be known. This expected channel gain can therefore be used to distribute resources like power and therefore there is no need for time adaptive allocation. A hardened channel also means linear signal processing like eigen beam forming (BF) and zero forcing (ZF) can be employed to precode and decode the signal. At the transmitter, the data sequence to be transferred is convolved with the conjugate of the time reversed version of the (channel state information (CSI). The data for the terminals is then added and fed to the antenna for transmission.

Another effect is that the thermal noise averages out to its expected value [12], [13]. The system essentially becomes interference limited. All sub-carriers in a wireless transmission system become equally good and users do not need to be scheduled in frequency domain. This means all users have access to the whole frequency domain available. This means higher data rate and link reliability become possible.

In massive MIMO base stations operate autonomously [13]. There is no cooperation among them when they do signal processing except for relatively slow tasks like power control and pilot allocation. TDD based Massive MIMO exploits the fact that the propagation channel is reciprocal in uplink and downlink directions. The time-frequency resources are split into what are called channel coherent intervals. The time-frequency coherent interval is basically the space within which the channel may be considered to be static. It is made up of the coherent bandwidth, B_c and coherence time T_c [23]. During the coherent time, the terminals send orthogonal pilots to the base station which in turn use these to estimate the channel responses. The BS uses the uplink channel responses to precode the downlink data so as to beamform the data to desired terminal location.

Non-linear precoding and detection systems can also be used for massive MIMO systems as they are optimal. They however do require more complex signal processing. Non-linear signal processing include dirty paper coding (DPC), vector pertubation (VP) and lattice methods as explained in [17].

As explained in [17], for massive MIMO linear precoders and detectors like matched filter (MF), zero forcing (ZF) and MMSE may be used for the massive MIMO signal. The channel vectors for all users need to be independent. Linear signal processing methods are however generally sub-optimal [5]. Each of the M antennas at the BS transmits a linear combination of symbols meant for k terminals in a cell. In [48], [30] and [42], the authors do compare the performance of the various linear precoding systems. Among other things, they compare the obtainable sum rate as a function of the number of antennas at the BS for a given number of terminals.

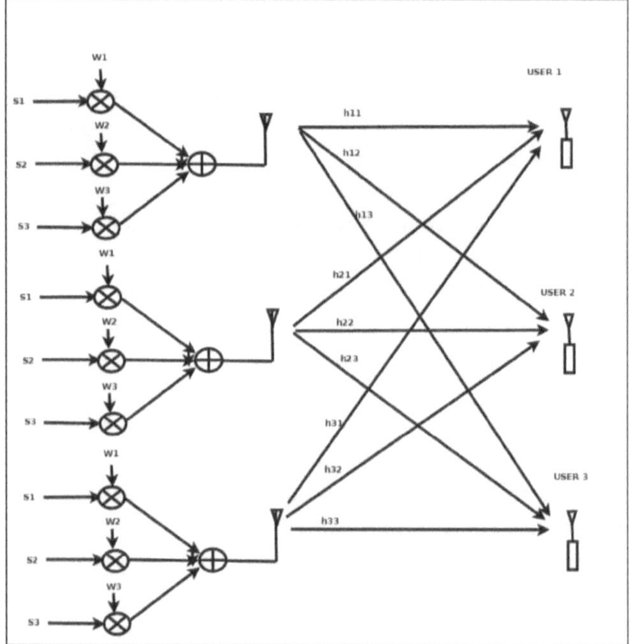

Figure 2.9: Massive MIMO

Some of the linear signal processing methods that can be used to precode and detect the signal at the terminals include the maximal ratio transmission (MRT), zero forcing, regularized zero forcing (RZF), matched filtering and eigen beamforming methods. A typical massive MIMO system may be as shown in Figure 2.9. These linear signal processing methods are known to be typically sub-optimal. Their performance can be benchmarked against non-linear signal processing methods like dirty paper coding and maximum likelihood (ML) methods [44], [19] which are known to be optimal. The next section discusses at the principle behind MIMO channel decomposition.

2.6.1 Transmitter Precoding

Precoding refers to preprocessing done to a signal at the transmitter using the channel state information at the transmitter (CSIT) in order to match the channel conditions [48]. A precoder decomposes the data to be transmitted into orthogonal spatial streams and allocate power to these spatial streams. The diagram in Figure 2.10 shows a typical precoding processing at the transmitter.

The transmitted data is generated by multiplying the input data by a transformation vector **T**. The precoded data is thus given by:

$$\mathbf{x} = \mathbf{T}\tilde{\mathbf{x}} \tag{2.12}$$

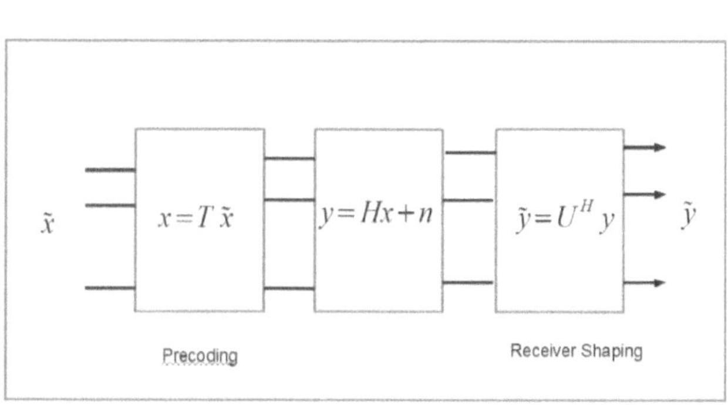

Figure 2.10: Precoding theory illustration: [47]

The received signal is given by:

$$\tilde{\mathbf{y}} = \mathbf{U}^H\mathbf{y} \tag{2.13}$$
$$= \mathbf{U}^H(\mathbf{Hx} + \mathbf{n}) \tag{2.14}$$
$$= \mathbf{U}^H(\mathbf{U\Lambda T}^H\mathbf{Hx} + \mathbf{n}) \tag{2.15}$$
$$= \mathbf{U}^H\mathbf{U\Lambda T}^H\mathbf{x} + \mathbf{U}^H\mathbf{n} \tag{2.16}$$
$$= \mathbf{U}^H\mathbf{U\Lambda T}^H\mathbf{T}\tilde{\mathbf{x}} + \mathbf{U}^H\mathbf{n} \tag{2.17}$$
$$= \mathbf{\Lambda}\tilde{\mathbf{x}} + \mathbf{U}^H\mathbf{n} \tag{2.18}$$
$$= \mathbf{\Lambda}\tilde{\mathbf{x}} + \tilde{\mathbf{n}} \tag{2.19}$$

where $\tilde{\mathbf{n}} = \mathbf{U}^H\mathbf{n}$. The transmit precoding and receiver shaping decompose the channel into R_H independent parallel streams. The MIMO system can support R_H times the data rate of one SISO channel. The precoding matrix $\mathbf{T}$ is a function of the channel matrix, $\mathbf{H}$. Precoding can be divided into linear and non-linear precoding. Non-linear precoding methods are complex to implement but are optimal solutions. Conversely non-linear precoding methods are simpler but mostly sub-optimal solutions. This study focuses more on linear precoding, which are more practically possible to implement. The next subsection briefly describes some of the linear precoding that may be employed for massive MIMO.

2.6.2   Linear Signal Detection

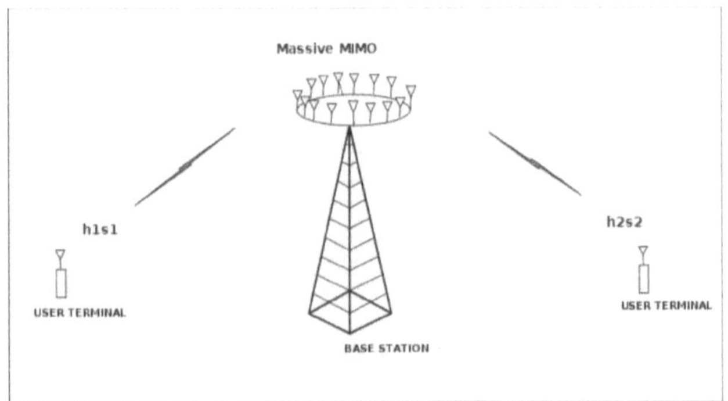

Figure 2.11: Massive MIMO detection principle for a two user case

Figure 2.11 shows a two user linear detection signal scenario. Assume two user terminals, user 1 and user 2 that are communicating with the Base Station (BS). Assume these two users are experiencing Rayleigh fading with independent and identically distributed (i.i.d) channels. Two signals meant for the two terminals are s_k for $k = 1, 2$. Assume we have M antenna elements at the Base Station. The two channel matrices for the two signals are given by

$$h_k = [h_{k1}, ..., h_{kM}]^T \sim \mathcal{N}(0, I_M) \tag{2.20}$$

The noise is also normally distributed and is given by:

$$n \sim \mathcal{N}(0, I_M)$$

The received signal is given by

$$y = h_1 s_1 + h_2 s_2 + n \tag{2.21}$$

For user 1, the terminal detects the signal using $v_1 = \frac{1}{M} h_1$

The received signal is given by:

$$\tilde{y}_1 = v_1^H y = v_1^H h_1 s_1 + v_1^H h_2 s_2 + v_1^H n \tag{2.22}$$

but

$$v_1^H h_1 = \frac{1}{M} \| h_1 \|^2 \tag{2.23}$$

where $\| h_1 \|^2$ is the inner product of the channel vector which is given by:

$$h_k^T h_k = [h_{k1}.....h_{kM}]^T [h_{k1}.....h_{kM}] \tag{2.24}$$

$$= h_{11}^2 + h_{12}^2 + ... + h_{kM}^2 \tag{2.25}$$

$$= \sum_{m=1}^{M} h_{km}^2 \tag{2.26}$$

As $M \to \infty$, for an i.i.d, the inner product of the channel response converges to the expected value of the square of any of the channel realizations. For illustration we can use h_{11}.

$$h_k^T h_k = \sum_{m=1}^{M=\infty} h_{km}^2 \tag{2.27}$$

$$= E[\|h_{11}\|^2] \tag{2.28}$$

$$= 1 \tag{2.29}$$

Thus the received signal can be expressed as

$$\tilde{y}_1 = s_1 + v_1^H h_2 s_2 + v_1^H n \tag{2.30}$$

Also

$$v_1^H h_2 = \frac{1}{M}\|h_1 h_2\| \xrightarrow{M \to \infty} E[\|h_{11}^H h_{21}\|] \tag{2.31}$$

This $v_1^H h_2$ converges to the mean value of the product of any two channel realizations, for example h_{11} and h_{21}. Since the two channels are independent, the expectation of their product is zero. Similarly the noise component also vanishes since it is independent of the signals sent. In reality the two channels may have some correlation and will not be exactly i.i.d distributed. However this fundamental assumption does simplify and justify the dramatic potential that massive MIMO offers. In sections that follow, specific linear detection techniques are presented.

2.6.3 Zero Forcing (ZF)

Zero Forcing Precoding

Zero forcing (ZF) precoding method is one of the most well researched linear precoding methods that may be applied in massive MIMO signal processing [24]. Figure 2.12 shows an illustration of a zero forcing precoding system. A ZF precoder, $\mathbf{T}$ in the diagram, is designed to minimize inter-symbol interference at the intended user. The precoder seeks to maximize such performance indicators as either throughput or fairness given specific power constraints.

In [44] the authors evaluated the performance of Zero Forcing and MMSE (Minimum Mean Square Error) precoding methods against the dirty paper coding which is non-linear and optimal. The authors were able to plot the spectral efficiency for the three precoding methods as a function of correlation for a 2 user scenario. The spectral efficiency decreases as the correlation increases for all precoding methods. For zero correlation between the users, the spectral efficiency was obtained was about 5 bps/Hz for all the three signal processing methods. At 0.9 correlation, DPC and MMSE spectral efficiency performance dropped to just less than 4 bps/Hz. ZF spectral efficiency dropped to a value just slightly above 0 bps/Hz.

The researchers in [44] also plotted the value of correlation of channels as a function of the number of base station antennas. Correlation was above 0.5 for two antennas and dropped to a value less 0.2 for 32 base station antennas. The researchers also plotted the ratio of obtained sum rates for MMSE and ZF to DPC sum rates as function of the number of base station antennas. They showed that for both ZF and MMSE, the sum rate approaches 1 as the number of antennas increases beyond 30 antenna elements.

In [29] the researchers looked at the performance of zero forcing in a MIMO system that uses the generalized inverse compared to the pseudo-inverse method. They argue that the generalized inverse is optimal and should give better results compared to the pseudo-inverse method which is known to be sub-optimal. The pseudo-inverse method can be used to maximize any desired performance measure. This could be sum rate or some fairness in power allocation to users. ZF is equivalent to power allocation to users under some constraints. The well-known water-filling algorithm can be used to do the power allocation for the user channels in a MIMO.

For zero forcing, nulls will be created for all other user terminals and a peak at the intended user terminal. In LOS environment, beams will be formed pointed in some desired directions. In NLOS waveforms that constructively reinforce will be formed at the desired terminal locations and destructively interfere elsewhere. In order to understand the spatial multiplexing gain obtained from MIMO, it is necessary to understand how the MIMO channel can be decomposed into independent parallel channels through which data may be sent.

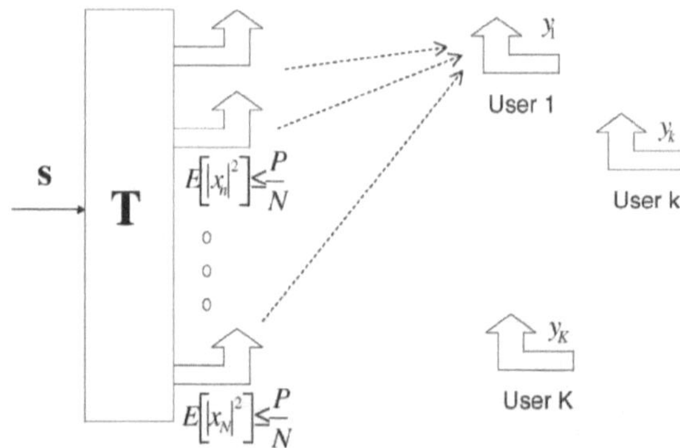

Figure 2.12: ZF precoder illustration with precoding matrix T [29]

Zero Forcing Equalization

ZF is a least squares approximation method which is employed to approximate the solution for an overdetermined linear system. This is the case when there are more equations than there are variables. For massive MIMO, there are more antennas at the transmitter than there are at the receiver. The linear system that relates the received signals $\mathbf{y}$, the transmitted signals $\mathbf{x}$, and the channel matrix $\mathbf{H}$ is an overdetermined linear system. ZF seeks to approximate the transmitted signals from the received noisy signals. The method seeks to minimize the square of the error between the received and the transmitted signals. It is thus called a least squares method. From the signal model earlier, this means minimizing the norm $||\mathbf{y} - \mathbf{Hx}||^2$.

$$||\mathbf{y} - \mathbf{Hx}||^2 = [\mathbf{y} - \mathbf{Hx}]^T[\mathbf{y} - \mathbf{Hx}] \tag{2.32}$$

$$= (\mathbf{y}^T - \mathbf{H}^T\mathbf{x}^T)(\mathbf{y} - \mathbf{Hx}) \tag{2.33}$$

$$= \mathbf{y}^T\mathbf{y} - \mathbf{H}^T\mathbf{x}^T\mathbf{y} - \mathbf{y}^T\mathbf{H}^T\mathbf{x} + \mathbf{H}^T\mathbf{Hx}^T\mathbf{x} \tag{2.34}$$

To find the minimum, means choosing $\mathbf{x}$ such that the differential of the norm with respect to $\mathbf{x}$ is zero.

$$\frac{d}{d\mathbf{x}}||\mathbf{y} - \mathbf{Hx}||^2 = 0 \tag{2.35}$$

$$-2\mathbf{H}^T\mathbf{y} + 2\mathbf{H}^T\mathbf{Hx} = 0 \tag{2.36}$$

$$\hat{\mathbf{x}} = (\mathbf{H}^T\mathbf{H})^{-1}\mathbf{H}^T\mathbf{y} \tag{2.37}$$

$\hat{\mathbf{x}}$ is used here to show that it is an approximation of $\mathbf{x}$. The quantity $(\mathbf{H}^T\mathbf{H})^{-1}\mathbf{H}^T$ is usually denoted $\mathbf{H}^\dagger$ and is called the pseudo-inverse. In [29] the authors do advocate for the use of a generalized inverse instead of the pseudo-inverse. They argue that the generalized inverse gives an optimal solution compared to the pseudo-inverse which is sub-optimal.

The channel matrix is generally composed of complex elements. Thus the corresponding pseudo-inverse is given by:

$$\mathbf{H}^\dagger = (\mathbf{H}^H\mathbf{H})^{-1}\mathbf{H}^H \tag{2.38}$$

where $(.)^H$ denotes the **Hermitian Transpose**.

Zero forcing is simple to implement but it however has a problem of amplifying the noise. ZF is very sensitive to the condition of the channel matrix. If the channel matrix smallest singular value is very small compared to the largest singular value, with the ratio approaching zero, the channel matrix is said to be ill-conditioned. The performance of ZF degrades. If otherwise, as the smallest to largest singular value ratio approaches 1, the channel matrix is said to be well conditioned and the performance of ZF improves. ZF needs high SNR values for it to perform well. At high SNR, it converges to MMSE equalizer which shall be discussed later.

2.6.4 Regularized Zero Forcing (RZF)

Direct inversion of the channel matrix as done in the ZF precoding method may lead to poor results when the channel matrix rank is low. In order to mitigate this, the regularized zero forcing method was designed. For RZF, the inversion of the channel matrix is regularized by adding a scaled identity matrix to $\mathbf{HH}^H$ before matrix inversion.

The precoding matrix is given by [45], [42]:

$$\mathbf{T}_{RZF} = \mathbf{H}^H(\beta\mathbf{I} + \mathbf{HH}^H)^{-1} \tag{2.39}$$

where β is the regularization factor.

2.6.5 Minimum Mean Square Error (MMSE)

The linear minimun mean square error (MMSE) MIMO equalizer and precoder utilize the Bayesian approach to estimating the transmitted signal vector $\hat{\mathbf{x}}$ from the observed signal vector $\mathbf{y}$ at the receiver. The assumed signal model is as given in equation 2.2. $\mathbf{H}$ is the channel matrix, while $\mathbf{n}$ is noise vector.

The MMSE estimator is the matrix $\mathbf{C}$, in equation 2.40 that minimizes the mean of the square of the error vector between the estimated signal vector $\hat{\mathbf{x}}$ and the transmitted signal vector $\mathbf{x}$

$$\hat{\mathbf{x}} = \mathbf{C}^{\mathbf{H}}\mathbf{y} \tag{2.40}$$

The MMSE estimator seeks to minimize the objective function below:

$$\mathbf{C} = \mathrm{argmin}_{\mathbf{C}} \mathbf{E}\{||\hat{\mathbf{x}} - \mathbf{x}||^2\} \tag{2.41}$$

$$= \mathbf{E}\{||\mathbf{C}^{\mathbf{H}}\mathbf{y} - \mathbf{x}||^2\} \tag{2.42}$$

where $\mathbf{E}$ is statistical the expectation. The cross covariance and covariance matrices for $\mathbf{x}$ and $\mathbf{y}$ are given by:

$$\mathbf{R_{xy}} = \mathbf{E}(\mathbf{xy^H}) \tag{2.43}$$

$$\mathbf{R_{yy}} = \mathbf{E}(\mathbf{yy^H}) \tag{2.44}$$

Differentiating equation 2.42 with respect to $\mathbf{C}$ and equating to zero gives the MMSE estimator as

$$\mathbf{C} = \mathbf{R_{yy}^{-1}R_{yx}} \tag{2.45}$$

Substituting $\mathbf{Hx} + \mathbf{n}$ for $\mathbf{y}$,

$$\mathbf{R_{yy}} = \mathbf{E}(\mathbf{HxH^Hx^H} + \mathbf{nn^H}) \tag{2.46}$$

$$= \mathbf{HR_{xx}H^H} + \sigma_{\mathbf{n}}^2\mathbf{I} \tag{2.47}$$

$$\mathbf{R_{yy}} = \mathbf{E}(\mathbf{yx^H}) \tag{2.48}$$

$$= \mathbf{HE}(\mathbf{xx^H}) \tag{2.49}$$

Taking consideration of the fact that noise is uncorrelated with the signal and assuming the unity for transmit power leads us to the final MMSE estimator as given by equation 2.51.

$$\mathbf{C} = \mathbf{H^H}(\mathbf{HH^H} + \sigma^2\mathbf{I})^{-1} \tag{2.50}$$

where $\mathbf{I}$ is an identity matrix while σ^2 is the noise variance. At high SNR values, MMSE converges to ZF equalizer while at low SNR it converges to the matched filter equalizer. The estimate $\hat{\mathbf{x}}$ is given by:

$$\hat{\mathbf{x}} = \mathbf{H}^{\mathbf{H}}(\mathbf{H}\mathbf{H}^{\mathbf{H}} + \sigma^2\mathbf{I})^{-1}\mathbf{y} \tag{2.51}$$

2.6.6 Maximal Ratio Transmission (MRT)

The precoding matrix for maximal ratio transmission is given equation 2.52 [30]. For MRT, weights are applied to the linear combination symbols for each antenna [44]. These weights are the complex conjugates of the channel realizations which would have been estimated from the uplink pilots. The resultant wave field will have peak power at the desired terminal location and will be zero elsewhere.

$$\mathbf{T}_{MRT} = c\mathbf{H}^{H} \tag{2.52}$$

where c is a constant used to normalize the precoding matrix and is given by:

$$c = 1/\sqrt{tr(\mathbf{H}^{H}\mathbf{H})} \tag{2.53}$$

where $tr(.)$ is the trace of the matrix.

2.6.7 Maximum Ratio Combining (MRC)

The maximum ratio combining (MRC) is a receive diversity scheme that coherently sums up weighted received signals from the multiple receive antennas. MRC enables the receiver to have what is called the diversity gain [47]. The diversity gain is the change in the bit error rate (BER) performance brought about by a diversity scheme. MRC tries to mitigate against the effects of both small scale and large scale fading. Figure 2.13 shows an MRC diversity scheme. The signal components ought to have experienced independent fading in order to get the diversity gain benefits. The multiple antennas at the receiver and the coherent combining of the signal components will increase the receiver signal to noise ratio (SNR) [47] compared to the single antenna case. This is called the array gain of the antenna array. The larger the array gain, the higher the obtainable spectral efficiency of the system. The signal components from the various antenna elements are multiplied by a complex signal α_n, whose magnitude is determined by the signal power of the particular branch. The obtained signals are then coherently added together.

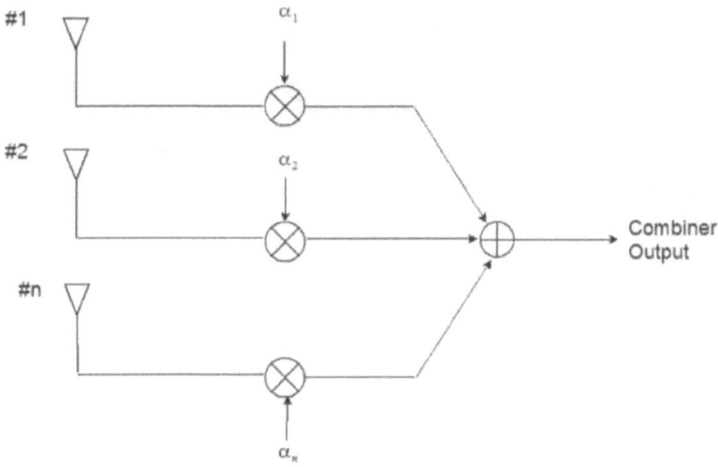

Figure 2.13: Maximal ratio combining

2.6.8 Eigen Beamforming

Figure 2.14 shows the eigen mode beam forming concept. Multiple signal beams are formed at the transmitter and receiver. Assuming knowledge of the channel at transmitter, a singular value decomposition (SVD) of the channel matrix is done. The signals to be transmitted are then also decomposed into an orthonormal space whereby each of the resultant basis vector is called an eigen beam. These eigen beams are matched to the channel eigen modes. The eigen beams are synthesized by weighting using the known channel values and summing them. Power can be split optimally among the obtained beams so as to maximize such criteria as throughput. This precoding method requires a rich scattering environment where distinct channel eigen modes can be obtained.

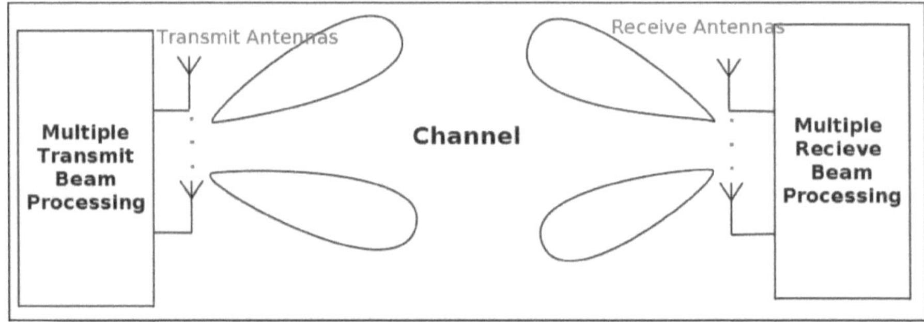

Figure 2.14: Eigen mode Precoding in MIMO

Eigen beamforming precoding is used with Matched Filtering (MF) for detection [42]. The precoding matrix is given by:

$$\mathbf{T}^{BF} = \tilde{\mathbf{H}}^{H}$$
(2.54)

where $\tilde{\mathbf{H}}^{\mathbf{H}}$ is the Hermitian transpose of the measured channel matrix.

2.6.9 Wiener Filter Precoding

The Wiener filter precoding method may also be used in massive MIMO. The Wiener filter seeks to minimize the mean square error between the desired and the observed signal. The Wiener filter seeks to solve the optimization problem below:

$$\{\mathbf{T}, \beta\} = \arg\min_{T,\beta} E[\|\mathbf{x} - \beta^{-1}\tilde{\mathbf{y}}\|^{2}]$$
(2.55)

subject to

$$E[\|\mathbf{Tx}\|^{2}] \leq \rho$$
(2.56)

where ρ signifies the signal to noise ratio, SNR.

The precoding matrix is given by :

$$\mathbf{T}_{WF} = \beta F^{-1}\mathbf{H}^H \tag{2.57}$$

where

$$F = \mathbf{H}\mathbf{H}^H + \frac{N}{\rho}\mathbf{I} \tag{2.58}$$

and $\beta = \sqrt{\frac{1}{tr(F^{-2}\mathbf{H}^H\mathbf{H})}}$, which can be interpreted as the optimal gain for the precoder and the channel and tr(.) is the trace of a matrix. N is the number of transmit antennas.

2.7 UL-DL Duality

The feasibility of massive MIMO lies in the ability to utilize uplink channel measurements for downlink transmission of the signal [28]. That means assuming that the uplink channel estimates are valid in the downlink direction. This is possible if we are using time division duplex (TDD) and is called the uplink/downlink duality. This brings about the fact that the receive combining vectors used for the various detection methods can also be used as the precoding matrices. The base station is thus able to listen to a particular direction of the UE.

2.8 System Model

This book analyzes spectral efficiency of massive MIMO systems in the uplink direction. A UE in a given random location transmits a random data signal to the BS. The signal transmitted by the UE can be modelled as:

$$s_k \sim \mathcal{N}(0, p_k) \tag{2.59}$$

The variance p is the transmit power of the signal or the average energy per sample. The channel response from a UE k to the BS is given by :

$$\mathbf{h}_k \sim \mathcal{N}(0, R_k) \tag{2.60}$$

where R_k is the channel auto-correlation, which is equivalent to the variance of the channel. The received signal at the BS is given by:

$$\mathbf{y} = \sum_{k=1}^{K} \mathbf{h}_k s_k + \mathbf{n} \tag{2.61}$$

where $\mathbf{n} \sim \mathcal{N}(0, \sigma^2 I_M)$, which is the Gaussian distributed noise zero mean and variance of σ^2. The summation in the equation represents the desired signals s_k which are filtered by the channel response h_k. The BS detects the signal using a particular detection method. The BS does this by correlating the received signal with a chosen receive combining method as shown in equation 2.62

$$\mathbf{v}_k^H \mathbf{y} = \mathbf{v}_k^H \mathbf{h}_k s_k + \sum_{i=k}^{K} \mathbf{v}_k^H \mathbf{h} s_i + \mathbf{v}_k^H \mathbf{n} \tag{2.62}$$

The right side of equation 2.62 has the desired signal, the intracell interference and noise components correlated with the receive combining signal $\mathbf{v}$. In reality, the BS uses estimated channel responses $\hat{\mathbf{h}}$. The BS uses a given estimation method to estimate the channel responses from the pilot signals. This work inherits MMSE estimation as was used in [28].

The MMSE estimator to the channel response $\mathbf{h}$ is given by [28] [page 249], as the vector $\hat{\mathbf{h}}$ that seeks to minimize the expectation of the square of the error value between the exact and estimated error i.e $E|\mathbf{h} - \hat{\mathbf{h}}|^2$. As proved in [28], the MMSE estimator is given 2.63.

$$\hat{\mathbf{h}} = \sqrt{p} R \Psi \mathbf{y} \tag{2.63}$$

where

$$\Psi = \left(\sum_{i \in P_i} p\tau_p R_i + \sigma_{UL}^2 I_M\right)^{-1}.$$

R is the channel correlation matrix, p is the uplink power and τ_p is the length of the pilot signal within coherent time.

From the described signal model the simulation environment can be designed. Applying the small scale and large scale effects to the transmitted signal allows us to receive it and estimate channel responses and then apply a selected receive combining method with a view to calculate the spectral efficiency (SE). The spectral efficiency is obtained from the well-known Shanon's theorem as:

$$SE = \frac{\tau_u}{\tau_c} E\{\mathbf{log_2}(1 + SINR_k)\} \tag{2.64}$$

where τ_u and τ_c represent the uplink portion of the coherent block and the total coherent block length respectively while $SINR$ is the signal to interference plus noise ratio and is given by:

$$SINR = \frac{p_k|\mathbf{v}_k^H \hat{\mathbf{h}}|^2}{\sum_{i=1}^K p_i|\mathbf{v}_K^H \hat{\mathbf{h}}_i|^2 + \mathbf{v}_k^H(\sum_{i=1}^K p_i\mathbf{C}_i + \sigma^2\mathbf{I}_M)\mathbf{v_k}} \tag{2.65}$$

where C_i represents the correlation matrix of the received signal given a set of channel estimates. The parameter p_k represents signal power while K is the number of user terminals.

2.9 Pilot Reuse

The pilot reuse factor is the number of cells that are using the same group of orthogonal sequences as pilots in the network. Figure2.15a shows an example of pilot reuse factor of 1 while Figure 2.15b shows an example of pilot reuse factor $f = 16$, for a 64 cell grid network. Cells that use the same pilots are said to be in the same pilot group.

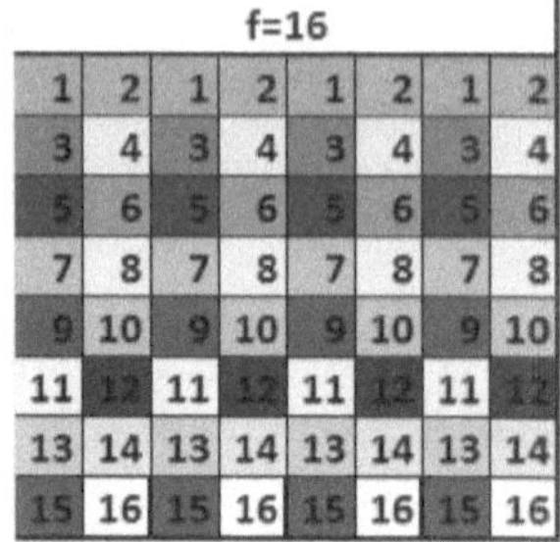

(a) Pilot Reuse factor f=1

(b) Pilot Reuse factor f=16

Figure 2.15: Pilot Reuse Examples

For a pilot reuse factor of 16 as in Figure 2.15b, that means there are 16 groups of cells, and each group uses the same sets of pilot sequences. With cells that use the same pilot sequences, it is possible that UEs may be allocated the same pilots, leading to what is called pilot contamination. As an extreme example with a pilot reuse factor of 64, each of the 64 cells have a different set of pilot sequences and therefore there is no pilot contamination. Another extreme example is for pilot reuse factor of 1, where all the cells use the same group pilot sequences. In this case there is a high level of pilot contamination. Given a pilot reuse factor f, it means the same pilot sequence is reused $\frac{1}{f}$ of the total number of cells.

Massive MIMO systems are able to estimate the channels using pilot signals. That estimation has to be done within the coherence block whose length is τ_c samples. If there are K users in a cell, then K pilots will be used per cell. That leaves $\tau - K$ samples to carry the actual data. If we increase the number of pilot reuse factor f, then the number of samples used to carry data τ_u is given by

$$\tau_u = \tau_c - fK \tag{2.66}$$

From equation 2.64, increasing f reduces τ_u and directly reduces the spectral efficiency. However, this also has the effect of improving the accuracy of channel estimation. This double effect of f on spectral efficiency can be analysed from simulation results for the effect of f on the spectral efficiency value. This work shall investigate the effect of pilot reuse size on the spectral efficiency of massive MIMO systems for linear signal processing methods.

2.10 Chapter Summary

This chapter discussed the concepts in traditional point to point MIMO, multi-user MIMO and finally leading to massive MIMO. The MIMO channel capacity theory was also explained. An important linear algebra concept called singular value decomposition that helps the parallel decomposition of the MIMO channel matrix was also explained. After that, various linear signal processing methods that can be applied to massive MIMO implementation were presented. The signal processing methods that this work is going to investigate are linear methods which are namely ZF, RZF, MR and MMSE precoding and receive combining. The linear signal processing methods are known to be sub-optimal compared to the non-linear methods like Dirty Paper Coding. The performance of the linear signal processing methods need to be investigated under massive MIMO regime. Spectral efficiency is one metric that can be used to measure performance. This chapter laid some background to the construction of a massive MIMO system which combine beamforming, phased array antenna and MIMO concepts. Lastly the theory for effect of pilot contamination on a massive MIMO system performance was analyzed. The foundation of this work was built from works already done as was cited in various literature.

Chapter 3

Methodology

3.1 Introduction

This section describes the methodology that is pursued in this study, which was designed with the aim to provide answers to the research questions given in section 1.5 in chapter 1. The methodology starts by looking at tools available to do this research. MATLAB software was chosen for the simulation. A structure of the simulation program that mimics a typical wireless environment was then constructed. An assumed signal model was developed and then some design algorithms were developed. Experiments were then set up in order to assess the performance of linear signal processing methods under various assumed channel conditions.

3.2 Methodology

In [41] the authors set up a channel sounding field measurements campaign to determine the obtainable sum rates for ZF and MMSE precoding schemes benchmarked against a precoding scheme called dirty paper coding (DPC), in an outdoor environment. They set up two measurement scenarios. The first scenario was based on the use of a vector network analyser (VNA). They connected port 1 of the VNA to the transmitter and port 2 to the receiver. At the transmitter side, a 200m optical cable was connected between the VNA port 1 and the power amplifier, with RF-to-optical and optical-to-RF converters in between. This represented the UE. The receiver consisted of an antenna array connected to port 2 of the VNA through a low noise amplifier (LNA). They used two types of antenna arrays, namely the cylindrical and linear arrays at the base station. The authors were able to get measured channel responses. The authors were thus able to calculate the sum rates for ZF and MMSE and compare with DPC precoding method. The second measurement scenario in [41] was based on the use of a channel sounder. They connected nine terminals through 200m cables to the transmitter sounder. They then connected an antenna array at the receive sounder. They were thus able to collect the measured channel responses and calculate sum rates for ZF, MMSE and DPC. For analysis they used Labview. The use of measurements done in a realistic environment is desirable. However for this current study, there was no such equipment available to perform the measurement campaigns.

In [28] the researchers built a MATLAB based simulation for massive MIMO. They assumed a 16 cell cellular network which are 250m x 250m. Base Stations were placed at the centre of each cell. For each UE they assume that it is served by the nearest base station. Of course in reality there may be obstructions, such that the UE does not necessarily always get served from the geographically nearest base station. Large scale fading was taken into consideration by assigning a median channel gain of -148.1dB at 1km and a pathloss exponent of 3.76 with standard deviation of 10 for the large scale fading. A bandwidth of 20MHz was assumed. This was done in order to make the simulation comparable to Long Term Evolution (LTE) which has a maximum bandwidth of 20MHz. A receive noise power of -94dBm was assumed. In both uplink and downlink, the transmit power assumed was 20dBm. A coherent block of 200 samples was assumed with pilot reuse factors of 1, 2 and 4. For small scale fading models, the researchers assumed a Rayleigh fading model. They assumed a Gaussian distribution for the signal angle of arrival about a given nominal angle which would have been calculated from the UE's relative position from the base station. The base station estimates the channel responses from the received pilot signal from the UEs it serves. They used the MMSE estimation method to estimate the received pilot signals. The assumption is that the base station assigns these pilots to UEs and therefore knows what pilot sequences a particular UE is using. The pilot sequences are ideally orthogonal. In time division duplex (TDD) mode, the estimated responses are valid for both the uplink and downlink. The authors were able to obtain the uplink and downlink sum rates for various receive combining schemes, assuming 10 UEs per cell and 10 to 100 antennas per base station. The approach taken in this current study is modelled along the approach in [28].

3.3   Requirements Analysis

This study, through the results of simulations, should provide insight into obtainable spectral efficiencies for various linear signal processing methods that may be employed in massive MIMO. The following steps will be done in order to get to the desired results.

- A simulation environment which can be implemented on an ordinary computer is to be used. The simulation should therefore not be too complex to be implemented in a computer. MATLAB was chosen as the simulation environment as it has a big library of functions and is relatively easy to use. In [41], the authors used field measurements while [28] used MATLAB.

- There should be a UE deployment mechanism in a given geographical area. A cell structure for the massive MIMO deployment should also be decided. As square cell structure like one in [28] was adopted.

- The UEs and base station communicate through the wireless channel. Propagation effects such as small scale fading and large scale fading of the wireless channel should therefore be modelled [28].

- A way to estimate channel responses in both UL and DL directions under the given propagation conditions should be obtained [4],[28]. For TDD based massive MIMO, channel responses obtained in the uplink are valid in the downlink, assuming the same time frequency coherent block as explained in [12],[13].

- Various linear signal processing methods should be employed and the respective spectral efficiencies shall be evaluated. References [28], [30], [35], [42], [39], [44], [43], [45] and [48] explain the linear signal processing methods applicable to massive MIMO.

3.4   Design of the simulation model

Three main scenarios were modelled in MATLAB. The first one was based on a single cell and a single base station as shown in Figure 3.1. The BS station location was fixed at (x, y) coordinates which were equivalent to (500m,500m) coordinates, which is the center of the cell. Twenty users were then randomly deployed in the $1000m$ x $1000m$ square cell. Figure

3.1 shows a snapshot of the users (UEs) deployed randomly in the cell. Under this scenario the spectral efficiency for linear receive combining and linear precoding signal processing methods were evaluated. The second scenario was built on a 4x4 cell grid network with 16 base stations and variable average number of UEs per base station as shown by a snapshot in Figure 3.2. The third scenario was built on 64 cell grid with 64 base stations as shown in Figure 3.3. Variable number of UEs could be deployed in the network. With more cells it was possible to evaluate the spectral efficiency performance as a function on both the number of antenna elements and pilot reuse factor. For a given snapshot, the distance to the nearest base station and the nominal angles to the base station could be calculated for each deployed UE.

Figure 3.1: UE and base station deployment in a single cell

3.5 Simulation Methodology

The flowchart in Figure 3.4 show the MATLAB simulation methodology employed. After distance and nominal angle values for UEs are determined, the corresponding channel gains due to large scale fading (shadowing) are determined. For an uncorrelated channel, a diagonal correlation matrix is obtained. For a correlated matrix, the correlation matrix is obtained. Channel estimation is then obtained. For this simulation, channel estimation was done using MMSE estimation. The same channel estimation method was used in all cases so as to be able to compare the effect of many antennas for the same receiver combining methods.

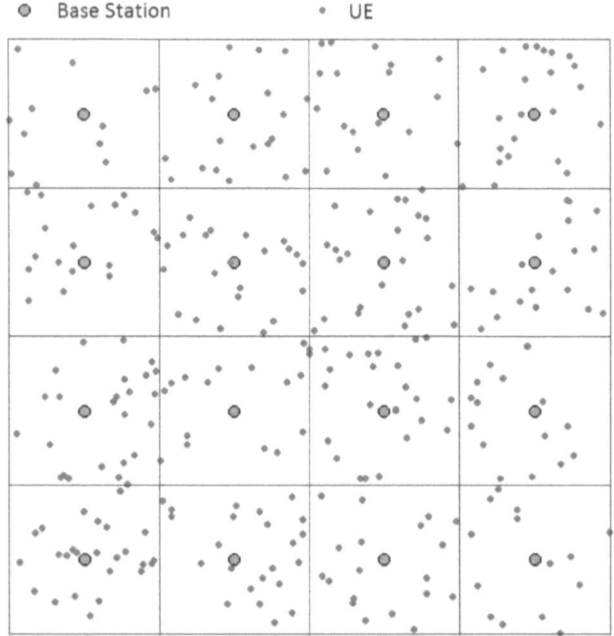

Figure 3.2: A snapshot for simulation 16 cell grid with UEs and BS locations

Antenna elements at the Base Station were varied. Single antennas user terminals were assumed. The resultant signal to interference ratio for each receive method was calculated. The corresponding spectral efficiency was thus determined. 100 Monte Carlo simulations were done, and the final result was an average of the 100 snapshots that were generated from random deployment of users within the cell. This process produced the averaged spectral efficiency as a function of the number of antenna elements assumed.

After channel estimation, microscopic channel vectors for the UEs are then obtained. Four receive combining methods were implemented in this study. The first to be implemented was MMSE, which is an optimal non-linear receive combining method. Three linear receiver combining methods, namely ZF, RZF and MR were then implemented so as to be able to benchmark their performance against MMSE. The three linear signal processing methods are known to be sub-optimal.

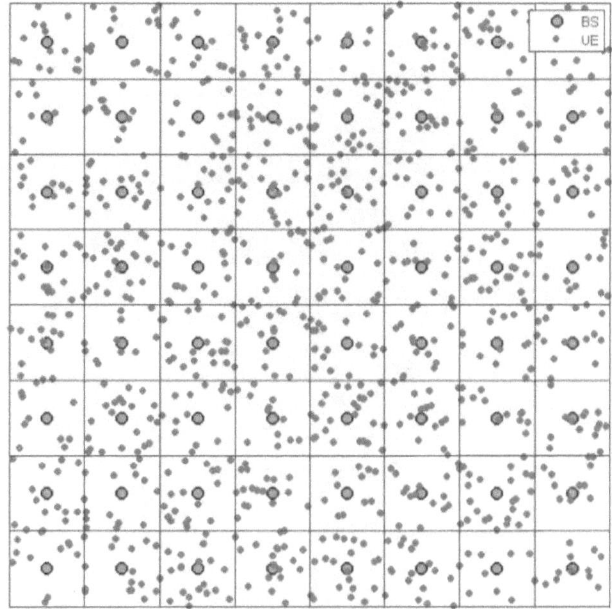

Figure 3.3: A snapshot for simulation 64 cell grid with UEs and BS locations

3.6 Single Cell Experiments: Experiment 1

The first group of experiments were performed using a single cell model network with one base station and 20 UEs. The experiments were divided into into two main groups. The first sub-group was to investigate the spectral efficiency performance of linear receive combining methods for a massive MIMO system. This sub-group was further divided into performance for an uncorrelated channel and a correlated Rayleigh fading channel. The second group was to investigate the spectral efficiency performance for linear precoding methods applicable to massive MIMO.

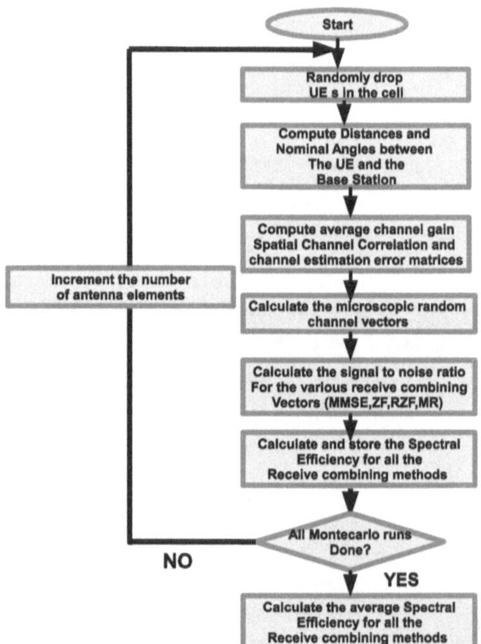

Figure 3.4: General Simulation Methodology for all experiments

3.6.1   Receive Combining For a Single Cell : Experiment 1a

For the first simulation experiment, the spectral efficiency four receive combining methods were to be investigated for an uncorrelated Rayleigh fading channel. These were MMSE, RZF, ZF and MR detection methods.

Effect of the Number of Antenna Elements on Spectral Efficiency

In massive MIMO, a large number of antenna elements is to be installed at the base station. As was noted in section 1.5 in chapter 1, it is important to investigate how the spectral efficiency of massive MIMO systems is affected by increasing the number of antenna elements at the base station while keeping the number of users constant. This simulation was done for a single cell. The simulation parameters are as described below.

Simulation Parameters

Table 3.1 shows the simulation parameters employed in this simulation. Small scale and large scale propagation propagation effects were modeled, with a shadow fading standard deviation of 10 degrees. This was assumed as recommended for a typical urban environment in [28]. The path loss exponent of 3.76 was assumed and a channel gain equivalent to -148.1 dB per 1000m was chosen. The coherence block, over which a channel may be assumed to be constant was assumed to be 200 samples long. The UE transmit power was assumed to be 20dBm. The choice of these parameters was chosen as recommended in [28].

Table 3.1: Simulation Parameters for single cell simulation

Simulation Parameters	
Parameter	**Value**
Number of BS or Cells	1
Number of UEs, K	10
Number of Antennas, M	10:100
Number of Simulations runs	100
Samples per coherence block, (τ_c)	200
UL transmit Power	20 dBm
Path loss Exponent, (α)	3.76
Channel gain at 1km	-148.1dB
Shadow fading Standard Dev, σ_{sf}	10
Cell Area	1km x 1km

3.6.2 Receive Combining For a Single Cell : Experiment 1b

For the second second simulation experiment under a 1 cell network model, a correlated Rayleigh fading wireless channel was assumed. The simulation parameters in Table 3.1 were used. The same linear receive combining methods were evaluated.

3.6.3   Precoding Simulation for a single cell : Experiment 1c

The third experiment was similar to the single cell receive combining experiment done earlier in Experiment 1a. The same simulation parameters that had been used in the receive combining experiment were used. The deployment of users in a square cell was the same. The algorithms to calculate the spectral efficiencies were the same. The receive combining vectors for MMSE, RZF, ZF and MR that had been used for receive combining were used as the precoding vectors.

3.7   16 Cell grid Experiments : Experiment 2

The first set of experiments in section 3.6 did not account for the effect on pilot contamination on the spectral efficiency performance of massive MIMO. This was because a single cell network model was used. In this section a multi-cell network which can account for the effects of pilot contamination was modelled.

3.7.1   Receive Combining : Experiment 2a

The second set of experiments were done in a 16-cell environment. A 16 cell network was designed. Figure 3.2 shows the design concept. The concept was in a way a replication of the first experiment already described. Each cell was 1kmx1km square. Base stations were placed at the centre of each square cell. An average of 20 UEs per base station were randomly deployed in each of the cells. A UE was assigned to the nearest base station within the grid. The UEs were assumed to be connected to the base station within their cell. Three particular scenarios were assumed. The first scenario was when the pilot reuse was 1. Pilot reuse of one means the number of pilots is equal to the number of UEs. The second and third scenarios where when the pilot reuse was 2 and 4 respectively. Pilot reuse of 2 means the number of pilot sequences available to UEs in a cell is twice the number of users. This means two sets of pilots are available for reuse. Similarly a pilot reuse of 4 was also designed. The four receive combining methods performance was then evaluated for the 16 cell grid network.

The simulation parameters for this experiment are as in Table 3.2. The other parameters were the same as in the one cell case in experiment 1.

Table 3.2: Simulation Parameters for a 16 cell grid network experiment

Simulation Parameters	
Parameter	**Value**
Number of BS or Cells	16
Number of UEs, K	10
Number of Antennas, M	20:200
Number of Simulations runs	100
Samples per coherence block, (τ_c)	200
UL transmit Power	20 dBm
Pathloss Exponent, (α)	3.76
Channel gain at 1km	-148.1dB
Shadow fading Standard Dev, σ_{sf}	10
Cell Area	1km x 1km

3.7.2 Precoding Simulation for 16 cell network : Experiment 2b

Under the 16 cell grid network, the second set of experiments was done to look at effect of pilot reuse on the performance of linear precoding schemes. The same simulation parameters that had been assumed for receive combining methods were adopted. The only change was the fact that receive combining vectors were used as precoding matrices for the four precoding methods being used in this work. These are MMSE, RZF, ZF and MR as before. Pilot reuse values of 1,2 and 4 were assumed and SE performances for the assumed pilot reuse factors were simulated for the 4 precoding methods.

3.8   64 cell model Simulation : Experiment 3

In section 3.7, the experiments were based on a 16 cell network model. With this 16 cell model some insights into the effect of pilot contamination could be obtained. In this section a bigger network model was designed. This could enable more analysis on the effects of pilot contamination to be obtained.

3.8.1   Receive Combining : Experiment 3a

The third set of experiments were done using a 64 cell grid. The 64 cell grid in Figure 3.3 shows the network model used throughout these experiments. An average number of UEs per base station was assumed. An average of 3 and 10 UEs per base station were assumed in these experiments. These numbers were arrived at after running the simulations and noting the number of UEs which would allow the simulations to be completed on the ordinary laptop that was used. In that sense they are arbitrary as different numbers could have been assumed.

Table 3.3: Simulation Parameters for a 64 cell grid network experiment

Simulation Parameters	
Parameter	**Value**
Number of BS or Cells	64
Pilot Reuse Factor	1,2,4,8,16,64
Average Number of UEs per BS, K	3, 10
Number of Antennas, M	16:65
Number of Simulations runs	100
Samples per coherence block, (τ_c)	200
UL transmit Power	20 dBm
Pathloss Exponent, (α)	3.76
Channel gain at 1km	-148.1dB
Shadow fading Standard Dev, σ_{sf}	10
Cell Area	1km x 1km

A 64 cell square grid as shown in Figure 3.3 was designed. Table 3.3 shows the simulation parameters employed in this simulation. The diagram in Figure 3.5 illustrates the pilot reuse factors used in these simulations. These pilot reuse factors were used for both receive combining and precoding simulations.

3.8.2   Precoding Simulation : Experiment 3b

The last set of experiments were done to evaluate the effect of the pilot reuse factor on the spectral efficiency of a massive MIMO system when using linear precoding signal processing. A 64 cell grid which had been used in Section 3.8.1 was used. MMSE, RZF, ZF and MR precoding were implemented. The pilot reuse factor was varied from 1 to 64. The same simulation parameters as in Table 3.3 were used.

f=1

1	1	1	1	1	1	1	1
1	1	1	1	1	1	1	1
1	1	1	1	1	1	1	1
1	1	1	1	1	1	1	1
1	1	1	1	1	1	1	1
1	1	1	1	1	1	1	1
1	1	1	1	1	1	1	1
1	1	1	1	1	1	1	1

f=2

1	2	1	2	1	2	1	2
2	1	2	1	2	1	2	1
1	2	1	2	1	2	1	2
2	1	2	1	2	1	2	1
1	2	1	2	1	2	1	2
2	1	2	1	2	1	2	1
1	2	1	2	1	2	1	2
2	1	2	1	2	1	2	1

f=4

1	2	1	2	1	2	1	2
3	4	3	4	3	4	3	4
1	2	1	2	1	2	1	2
3	4	3	4	3	4	3	4
1	2	1	2	1	2	1	2
3	4	3	4	3	4	3	4
1	2	1	2	1	2	1	2
3	4	3	4	3	4	3	4

f=8

1	2	1	2	1	2	1	2
3	4	3	4	3	4	3	4
5	6	5	6	5	6	5	6
7	8	7	8	7	8	7	8
1	2	1	2	1	2	1	2
3	4	3	4	3	4	3	4
5	6	5	6	5	6	5	6
7	8	7	8	7	8	7	8

f=16

1	2	1	2	1	2	1	2
3	4	3	4	3	4	3	4
5	6	5	6	5	6	5	6
7	8	7	8	7	8	7	8
9	10	9	10	9	10	9	10
11	12	11	12	11	12	11	12
13	14	13	14	13	14	13	14
15	16	15	16	15	16	15	16

f=64

1	2	3	4	5	6	7	8
9	10	11	12	13	14	15	16
17	18	19	20	21	22	23	24
25	26	27	28	29	30	31	32
33	34	35	36	37	38	39	40
41	42	43	44	45	46	47	48
49	50	51	52	53	54	55	56
57	58	59	60	61	62	63	64

Figure 3.5: The 64 cell grid Network Model Pilots

3.9 Discussion of the Methodology

The experiments described above will give insights into the performance of massive MIMO linear signal processing detection methods. The linear detection methods used were known sub-optimal [18]. The key metric to be used was the Spectral Efficiency (SE) obtained as a function of the number of antennas at the base station and the various pilot reuse factors assumed. From the obtained spectral efficiency plots, the obtainable spectral efficiency values for a particular number of antennas shall be obtained. This will determine whether massive MIMO enables the wireless system to obtain high SEs beyond legacy networks like LTE. Both large scale and small scale propagation effects were considered. Analysis was done for both receive combining in the uplink direction and precoding methods applied in the downlink direction. The effect of pilot contamination was to be studied using multi-cell grid networks in the form of a 16 and a 64 cell grid networks.

3.10   Chapter Conclusion

This Chapter looked at the general design methodology for the simulations which were to be carried out in this research. Three network models were designed. The first network model was based on a single cell network. User terminals (UE) were to be randomly distributed in a cell. Several snapshots were taken and the resulting spectral efficiency values averaged. This model was used to investigate the spectral efficiency of receive combining methods for a correlated and uncorrelated Rayleigh channel. The model was also used to investigate the spectral efficiency for linear precoding algorithms. The second network model was based on a 16 cell grid network model. The second set of experiments were based on this model. Both receive combining and precoding algorithms were to be investigated. The effect of pilot reuse factor could also be evaluated. The last network model was a 64 cell grid network model upon which the third set of experiments was based on. The effect of pilot contamination was to be more fully evaluated using this model.

A general increase in the spectral efficiency was expected to increase with more antenna elements at the base station. However the main aim was to see the relative performance of the linear signal processing methods against each other. The importance of increasing the number of antennas could therefore be observed. In addition, the performance of various signal processing methods were also evaluated against angular spread observed at the users. The simulations for the performance of linear signal processing receive combining and precoding algorithms were to be done in MATLAB.

Chapter 4

Results and Discussion

This Chapter presents results that were obtained from the simulations done. The results are divided into three main sections. The first group was based on a single cell. The second and third groups were based on a 16 cell grid and a 64 cell grid networks respectively. The simulation experiments were numbered 1a up to 3b as shown in Figure 4.1.

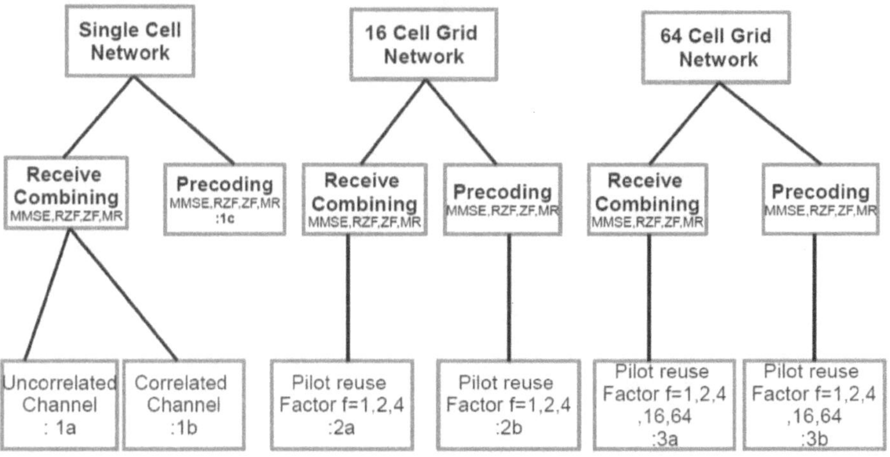

Figure 4.1: The layout of all simulation experiments done

Each of the three groups of experiments was divided into receive combining and precoding experiments. Experiments for receive combining methods for the single cell scenario had additional correlated/uncorrelated wireless channel scenario investigated. The rest of the experiments were all based on a correlated channel which is more likely than an uncorrelated channel. For simulations in Experiments 2 and 3, the pilot reuse factor was also varied for all signal processing methods that were investigated. The rest of this chapter will present the results for each experiment done.

4.1 Single Cell Simulation Results : Receive Combining Experiment 1

This section presents the simulation results obtained for a single cell network. It focuses on spectral efficiencies obtained as the number antenna elements were increased at a massive MIMO base station. For the first two experiments 1a and 1b, the effect of the wireless channel correlation is also investigated. The last experiment under this section investigated the spectral efficiencies obtained for precoding signal processing.

4.1.1 Receive Combining Simulation : Experiment 1a

The first experiment sought to obtain the achievable spectral efficiency for massive MIMO systems that use linear detection methods. The experiment was to tell the asymptotic behavior of the spectral efficiency as a function of antenna elements for four linear detection methods. Ideally the massive MIMO channel is uncorrelated. This implies that all the channel responses are independent and don't interfere with one another. It will therefore be easy to distinguish the MIMO channels at the receiver. The channel matrix will be a diagonal matrix such that the sum rate of the channel can be optimized to maximize the channel capacity or SE of a wireless system under given power constraints. Waterfilling is a popular power allocation algorithm for such optimization [17]. This is the propagation channel assumed for the first experiment. This experiment was restricted to analyzing the spectral efficiency in the uplink direction only.

The four receive combining schemes that were evaluated were the minimum mean square error (MMSE), zero forcing (ZF), regularized zero forcing (RZF) and maximal ratio (MR) combining methods. The four receive combining methods are linear but sub-optimal. Figure

4.2 and Figure 4.3 show the spectral efficiency trends of all the four receive combining methods as a function of the ratio between the number of antennas and the users in the cells. Figure 4.2 shows the trends for the 95% confidence intervals for SE values obtained from Monte Carlo simulations. Figure 4.3 gives the pictorial view of the SE trends obtained with the associated error bars for each SE value obtained shown. The error bars were calculated from the formula below:

$$\sigma_{\bar{x}} = \frac{\sigma}{\sqrt{n}} \tag{4.1}$$

where σ is the standard deviation of the population and n is the size (number of observations) of the sample.

Table 4.1 shows the maximum and minimum SE values obtained for the simulation of the four receive combining methods considered. The starting point was when the number of users in a cell was equal to the number of antenna elements at the BS. For this experiment, that means 10 antenna elements and 10 users per cell were assumed. Under the described propagation conditions, detecting the signal using MR managed to yield just less than 25 bits/s/Hz/cell. As antenna elements were incremented in steps of 10 while keeping the number of users constant, the spectral efficiency for MR gradually increased up to just above 25 bit/s/Hz/cell. This point corresponds to 100 antenna elements.

For this experiment, ZF initially had the worst spectral efficiency figure for the initial 10 antenna elements scenario considered. From the graph in Figure4.2 and Figure 4.3, increasing the number of antenna elements had the greatest effect on increasing ZF spectral efficiency compared to the three other receive combining methods. By the point when the number of antenna elements had doubled compared to the number of users in a cell, the SE performance for ZF had exceeded that for MR. RZF and MMSE had the best spectral efficiency performance as a function of antenna elements at the base station. It is notable however that, when the number of antenna elements reaches about 40, the performance of ZF had caught up with MMSE and RZF. These trends do show that ZF performance asymptotically approaches optimal performance as more antenna elements are added.

Table 4.1: Spectral Efficiencies for the uncorrelated Channel

Max Antenna/Users Ratio	minimum SE	maximum SE
MR	5	25
ZF	0	190
RZF	25	190
MMSE	25	190

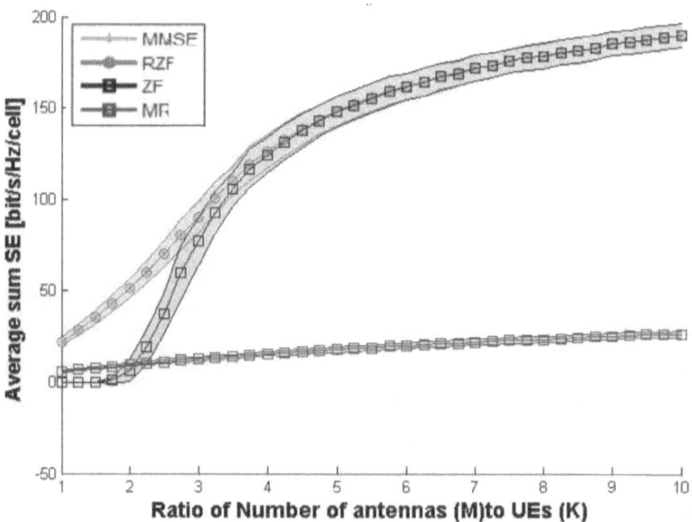

Figure 4.2: Spectral Efficiency for an uncorrelated channel

4.1.2   Receive Combining Simulation : Experiment 1b

The second experiment was done assuming a correlated propagation channel model. In reality wireless propagation channels are likely to have some level of correlation. The channel matrix is not diagonal and fading experienced by different paths is to some extent correlated. A Rayleigh correlated channel was thus assumed. The same receive combining methods, namely MR, ZF, RZF and MMSE were used to detect the receive signal at the base station. The results were as shown in Figure 4.4, Figure 4.5 and Table 4.2. As in the first experiment, only the uplink was considered.

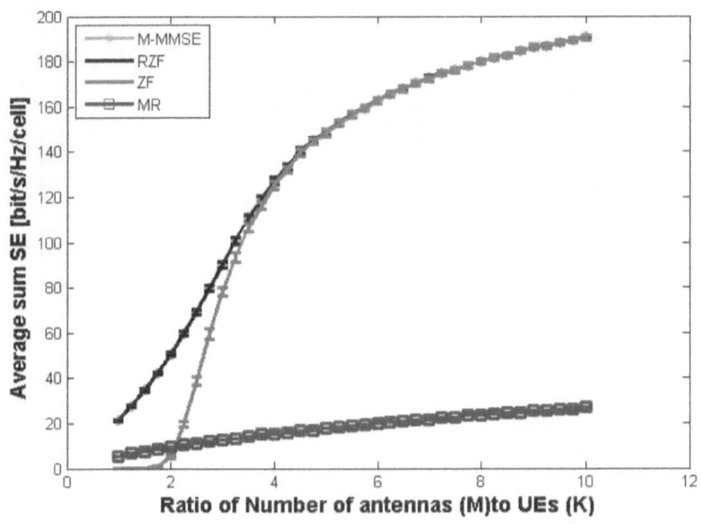

Figure 4.3: Spectral Efficiency for an uncorrelated channel

MR had the worst performance of all the four detection methods. As antenna elements were increased while keeping users constant, the spectral efficiency for all the signal processing methods began to increase. The spectral efficiency for MR started at about 13 bits/s/Hz/cell and ended at about 50 bits/s/Hz/cell. All the other receive combining methods ended at about 180 bits/s/Hz/cell.

Beyond 30 antenna elements, all detection methods managed to converge except for MR. An interesting point is that, the initial SE performance when the number of antenna elements was the same as the users in a cell, the correlated channel performed better than the uncorrelated channel. However as the ratio of antenna elements to users increased, the uncorrelated channel performed better as was expected.

Table 4.2: Spectral Efficiencies for the correlated channel

Max Antenna/Users Ratio	minimum SE	maximum SE
MR	13	47
ZF	55	178
RZF	78	178
MMSE	78	178

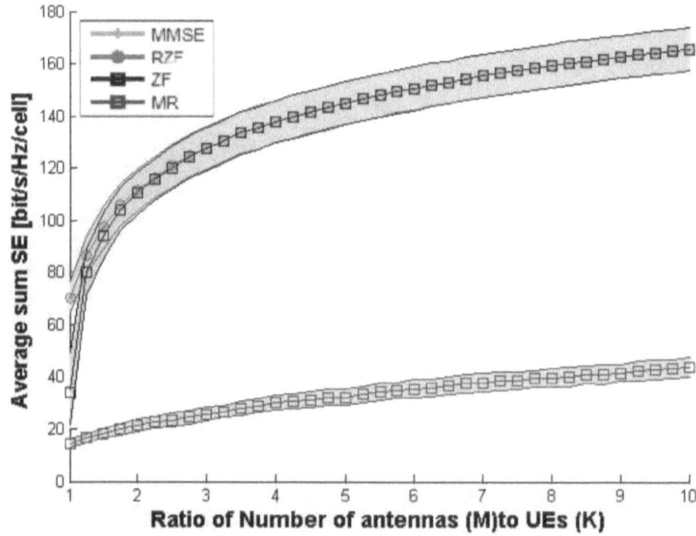

Figure 4.4: Spectral Efficiency for an correlated Channel

4.1.3 Precoding Simulation : Experiment 1c

Using the UL/DL duality principle, the same receive combining vectors were used as the corresponding precoding matrices. Figure 4.7 shows the spectral efficiency results for the various procoding methods. As was done in the UL case, a single cell scenario was the first case to be analyzed. Four precoding schemes were considered. These are MMSE, RZF, ZF and MR. As shown in Figure 4.7, the simulation results showed the same trends that had been obtained for the corresponding UL single cell scenario simulated earlier. All precoding schemes monotonically increased their spectral efficiency trends as the ratio of number of antennas to users in a cell were increased from 1 to 10. MSSE and RZF performed equally well as was the case for receive combining. When the number of antennas was equal to the number of users, ZF precoding performed worse than MMSE and RZF. As the number of antennas was increased ZF almost caught up with both MMSE and RZF by the point when the ratio was 10. MR precoding also increased monotonically, but at the slowest pace compared to the other precoding schemes. Also observed was that the overall spectral efficiency for precoding was much less than that for receive combining.

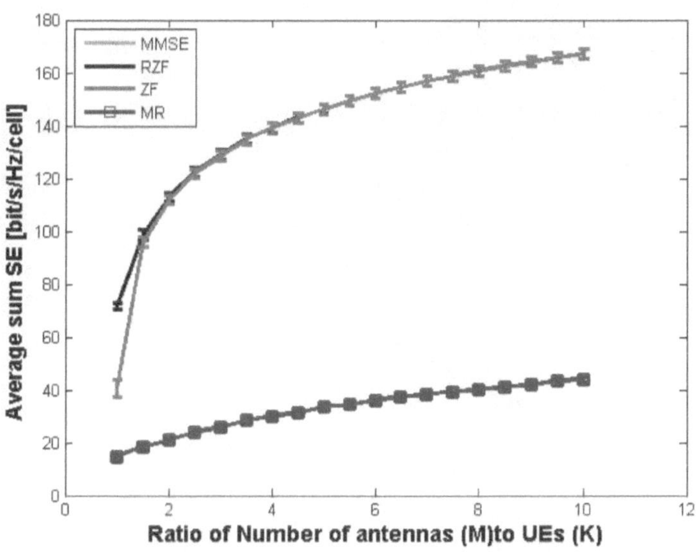

Figure 4.5: Spectral Efficiency for a correlated Channel

Table 4.3: Spectral Efficiency for 1 cell precoding system

Max Antenna/Users Ratio	minimum SE	maximum SE
MR	1.6	11
ZF	1	17
RZF	78	18
MMSE	78	18

4.2 16 Cell Grid Simulation Results : Experiment 2

The second group of experiment was done using a 16 cell grid network. Both precoding and receive combining spectral efficiencies were investigated for various values of pilot reuse factors.

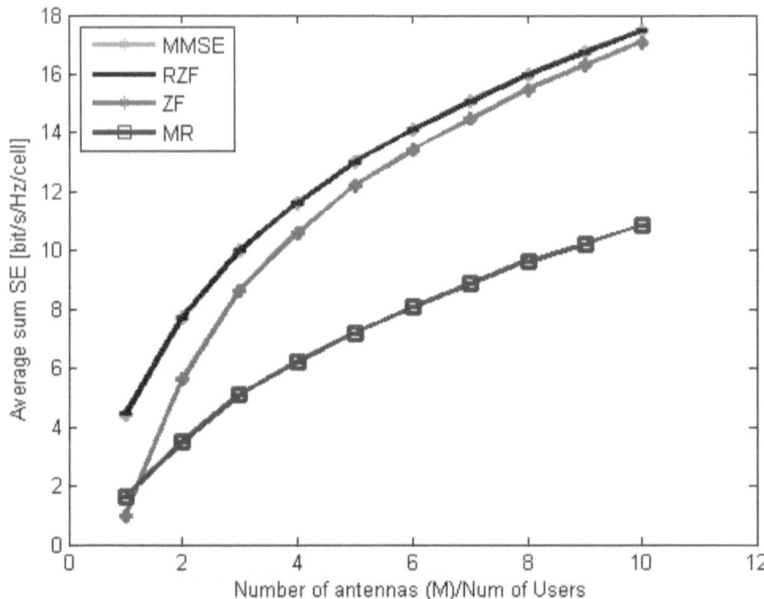

Figure 4.6: DL Spectral Efficiency for 1 Cell

4.2.1   Receive Combining Simulation : Experiment 2a

The results in Figure 4.8 through Figure 4.9 show the spectral efficiency trends obtained as the pilot reuse was varied from 1, 2, 4 and 8 in a 16 cell grid setup. The overall asymptotic behavior, as larger antenna arrays were assumed, was similar to the single cell scenario for all signal processing methods. However the values for spectral efficiency were correspondingly lower for the 16 cell scenario compared to the single cell case. For MMSE, reuse factor 4 yielded a corresponding 10% degradation in maximum SE when the number of antenna elements is 100 compared to the reuse factor of 2. This is in comparison to the case when 10 antenna elements are used for 10 users where the degradation in spectral efficiency was 26%.

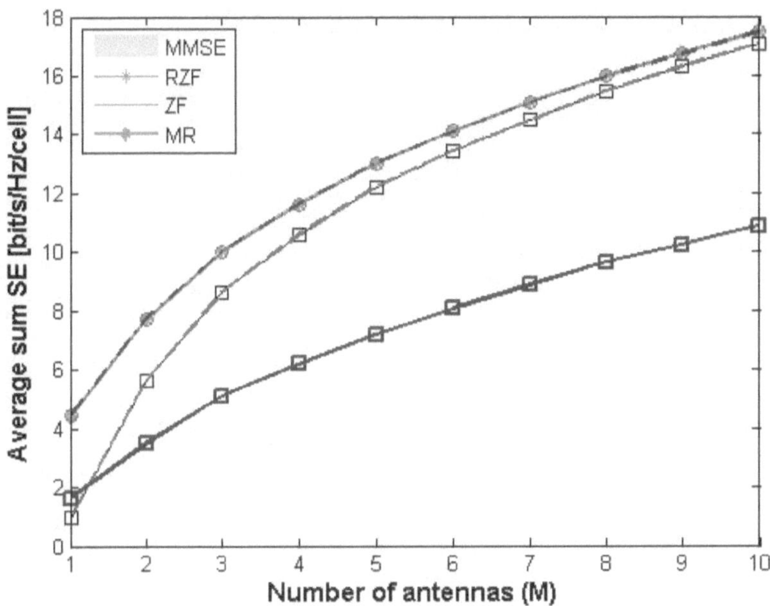

Figure 4.7: DL Spectral Efficiency for 1 Cell

4.2.2 Precoding Simulation : Experiment 2b

As was done for the receive combining scenarios, the next simulation experiment assumed a 16 cell cellular environment. Pilot reuse factors were also varied between reuse factor of 1, 2, 4 and 8. The results obtained are as shown in Figure ?? through Figure 4.11. Similar asymptotic behavior with the corresponding receive combining signal processing methods was observed. MMSE and RZF would perform better but with more antennas ZF would catch up. MR precoding also improved with more antennas but would not catch up with the other precoding schemes even when 100 array antenna size was adopted. The effect of pilot contamination was less pronounced for precoding schemes. The SE trends obtained with pilot reuse factor 1 was only marginally higher than that for pilot reuse factor 2, 4 and 8.

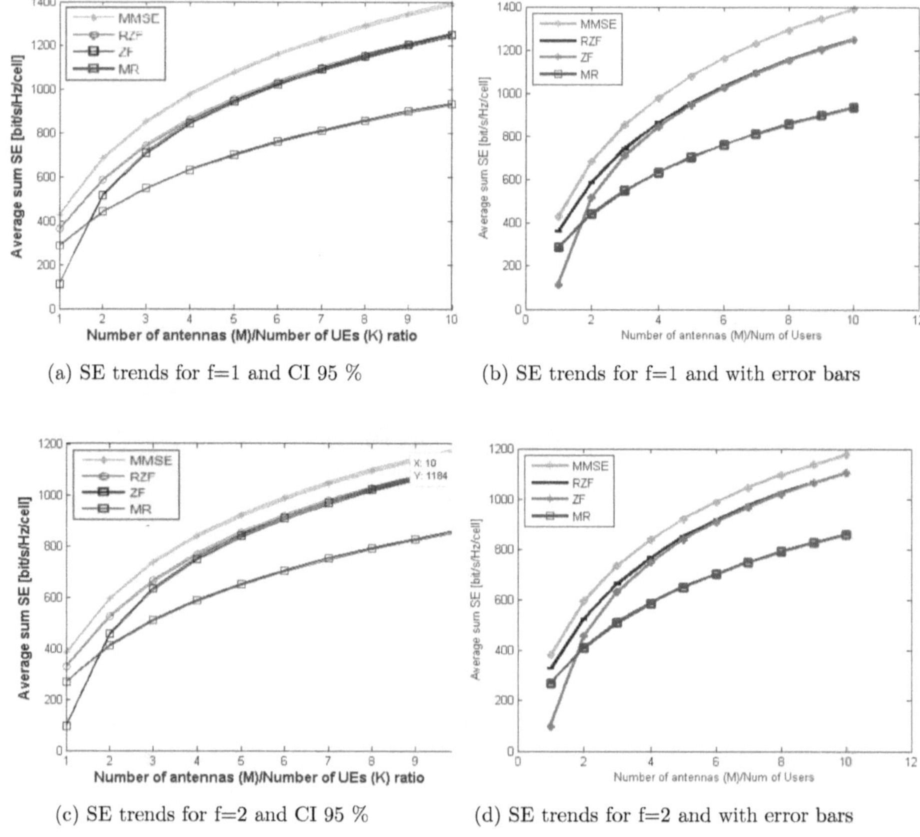

(a) SE trends for f=1 and CI 95 %

(b) SE trends for f=1 and with error bars

(c) SE trends for f=2 and CI 95 %

(d) SE trends for f=2 and with error bars

Figure 4.8: Effect of Pilot Reuse factors on Spectral Efficiency:Receive Combining

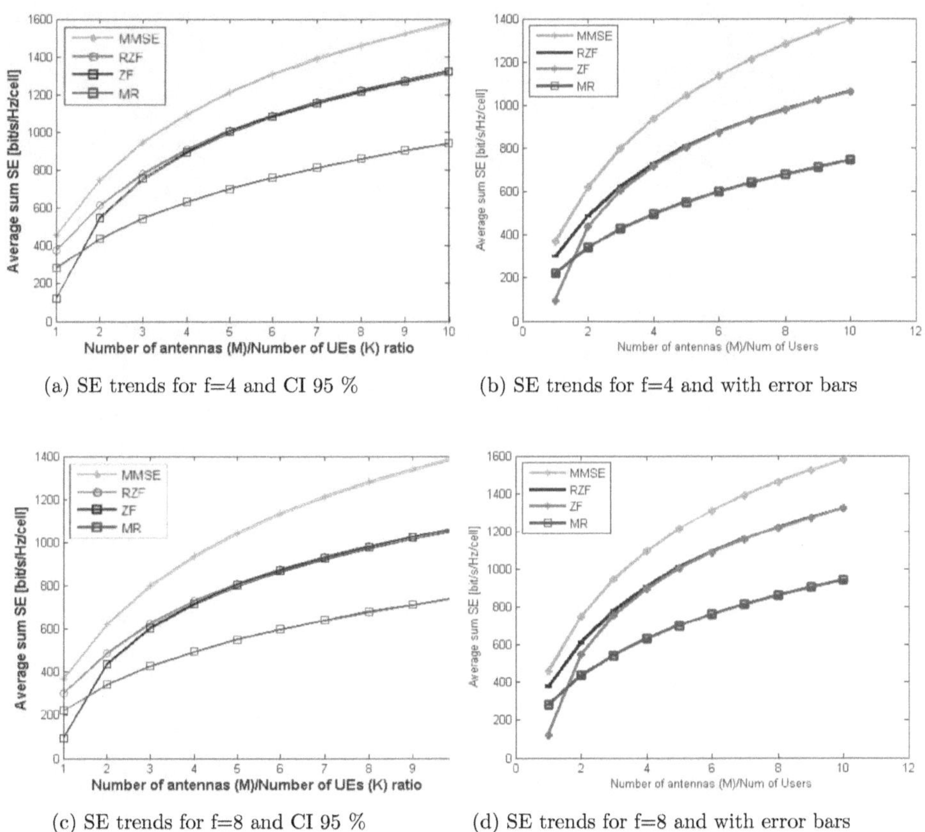

(a) SE trends for f=4 and CI 95 %

(b) SE trends for f=4 and with error bars

(c) SE trends for f=8 and CI 95 %

(d) SE trends for f=8 and with error bars

Figure 4.9: Effect of Pilot Reuse factors on Spectral Efficiency:Receive Combining Methods

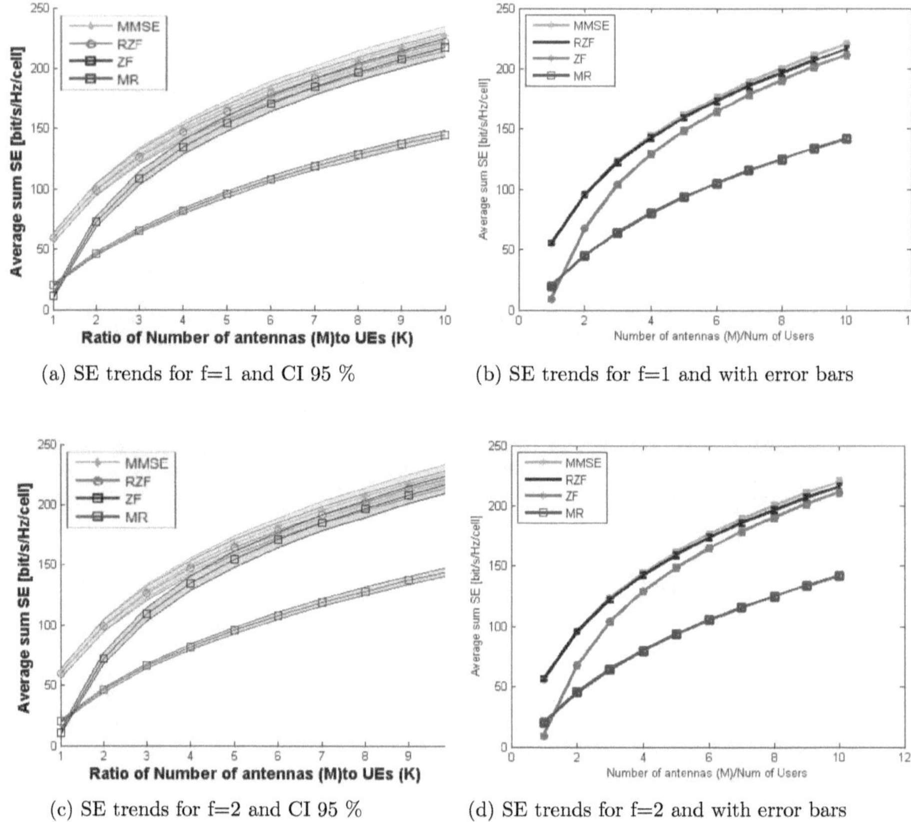

(a) SE trends for f=1 and CI 95 %

(b) SE trends for f=1 and with error bars

(c) SE trends for f=2 and CI 95 %

(d) SE trends for f=2 and with error bars

Figure 4.10: Effect of Pilot Reuse factors on Spectral Efficiency:Precoding Methods

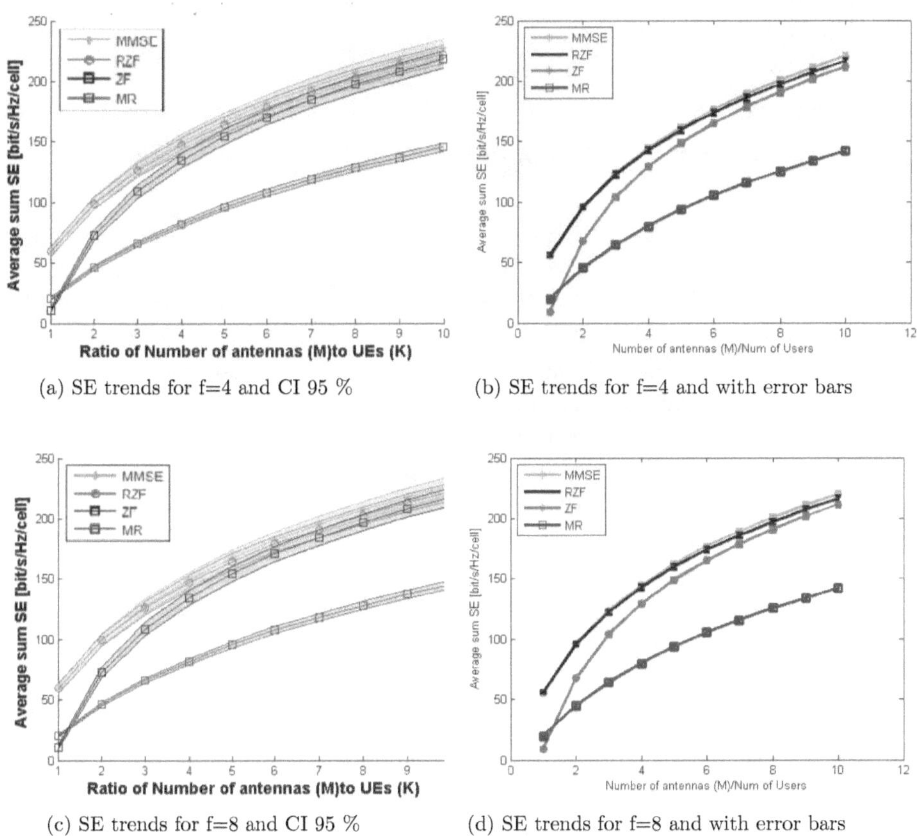

(a) SE trends for f=4 and CI 95 %

(b) SE trends for f=4 and with error bars

(c) SE trends for f=8 and CI 95 %

(d) SE trends for f=8 and with error bars

Figure 4.11: Effect of Pilot Reuse factors on Spectral Efficiency:Precoding Methods

4.3   64 Cell Grid Network: Experiment 3

The third group of experiments sought to investigate the effect of the pilot reuse factor on the spectral efficiency of a massive MIMO network. By having a bigger network compared to the previous ones of 1 and 16 cells, it was possible to obtain more values of pilot reuse factor, and investigate its impact.

4.3.1   Receive Combining Simulation : Experiment 3a

Figure 4.12 through Figure4.13 show the obtained spectral efficiencies for the 64 base stations with an average of 10 UEs per cell. The graphs in Figure 4.12a and Figure 4.12b show the spectral efficiencies obtained for MMSE, RZF, ZF and MR receive combining methods for the pilot reuse factor of 1. All receive combining methods showed an improvement in the obtainable spectral efficiency values as antenna elements per base station were increased from 10 to 100. MMSE had the best performance as it increased from about 15 b/s/Hz to 35 b/s/Hz. RZF had the next best performance, although it was initially less than MR. With more antenna elements added, ZF surpassed MR by the point when just more than 20 antenna elements per base station was assumed. By the point when antenna elements per base station had surpassed 35, the performance of ZF was equal to that of RZF. With few antenna elements MR performed better than ZF and RZF. However as antenna elements were increased, MR performance was surpassed by all other three receive combining methods. Similar trends were obtained for pilot reuse factors 2, 4 and 8.

4.3.2   Receive Combining Simulation : Experiment 3b

Pilot reuse sizes greater than 8 could not be used for a 16 user cells as the pilot sizes would exceed the assumed coherent block size of 200 samples. Fewer users per base station needed to be assumed in order to be able to investigate the use of more pilot reuse sizes. Pilot reuse sizes up to 64 were investigated using an average of 3 users per cell for each receive combining method. Figure 4.14a through Figure 4.14d show the variation of the obtained spectral efficiency as a function of the pilot reuse size as well as the average number of antennas per base station in the 64 cell grid network. Each graph is a trend realization

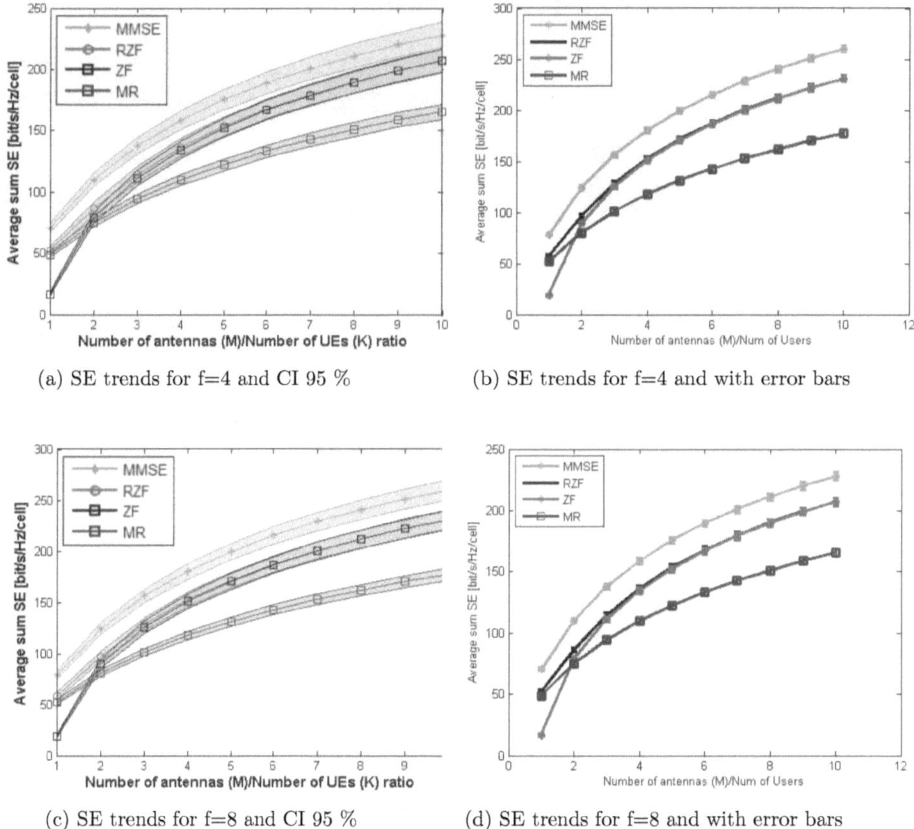

(a) SE trends for f=4 and CI 95 %

(b) SE trends for f=4 and with error bars

(c) SE trends for f=8 and CI 95 %

(d) SE trends for f=8 and with error bars

Figure 4.12: Effect of Pilot Reuse factors on Spectral Efficiency:Receive Combining Methods

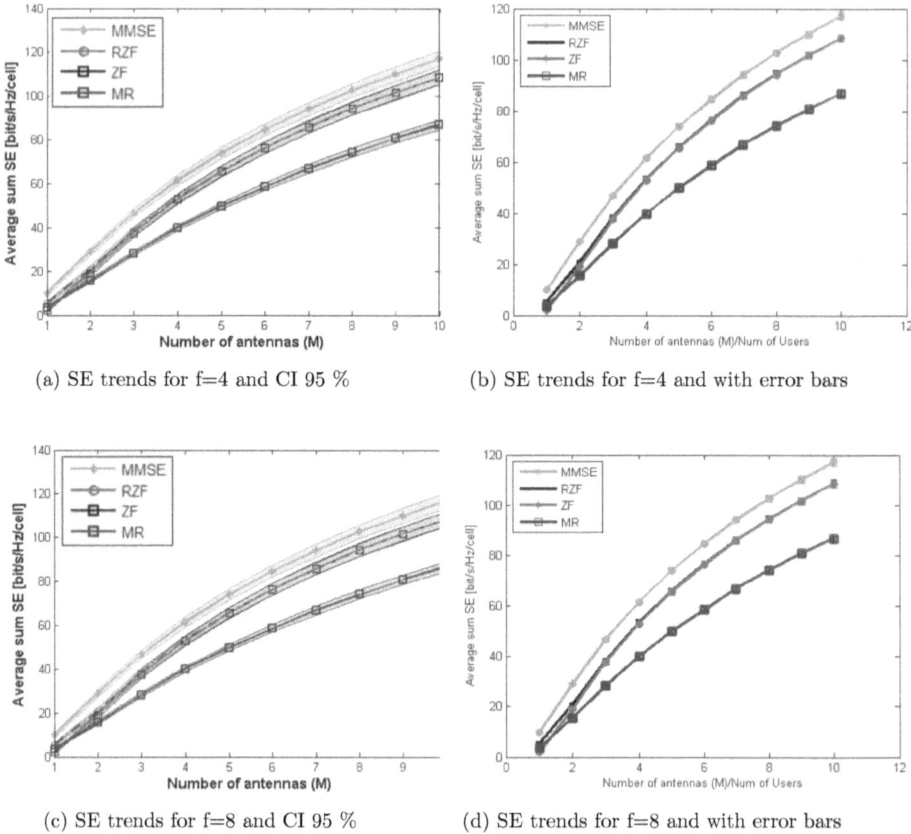

(a) SE trends for f=4 and CI 95 %

(b) SE trends for f=4 and with error bars

(c) SE trends for f=8 and CI 95 %

(d) SE trends for f=8 and with error bars

Figure 4.13: Effect of Pilot Reuse factors on Spectral Efficiency:Receive Combining Methods

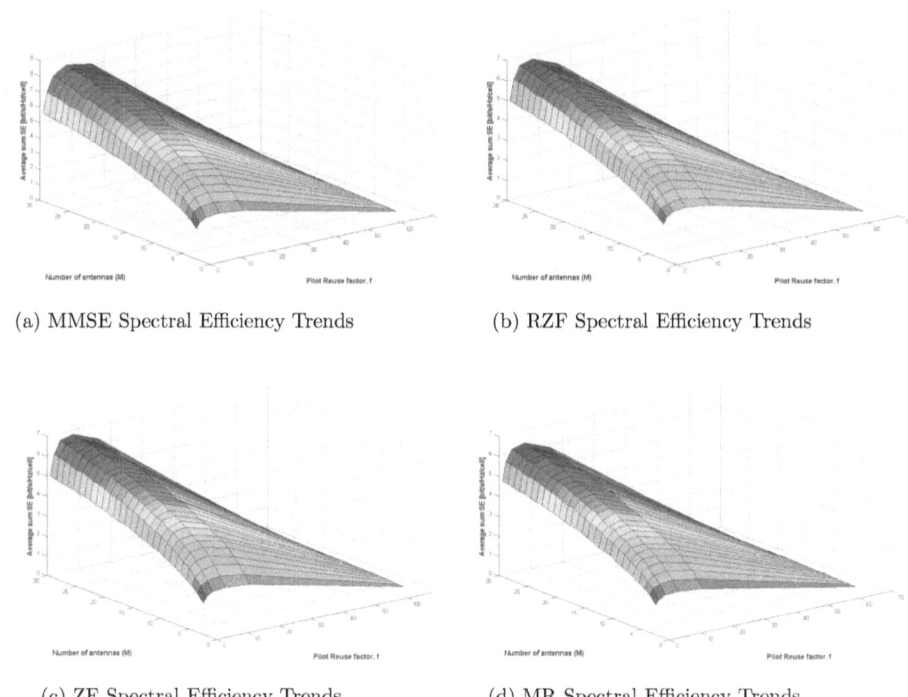

(a) MMSE Spectral Efficiency Trends

(b) RZF Spectral Efficiency Trends

(c) ZF Spectral Efficiency Trends

(d) MR Spectral Efficiency Trends

Figure 4.14: Effect of Pilot Reuse factors on Spectral Efficiency:Receive Combining Methods

for one of the four receive combining methods in this study. As shown in all graphs, the spectral efficiency increases from the point when pilot reuse is 1 until when it is 8. It peaks at the point when pilot reuse is 8 and then starts decreasing for pilot reuse sizes of 16 and 64. From these graphs reuse factor of 8 was the optimum value in order to maximize the spectral efficiency obtained. If the pilot reuse factor is high, estimation of the channels becomes more accurate but less samples will be available to carry the user data. The optimal value is a compromise between needing to obtain accurate channel estimates and transmitting as many data carrying samples as possible for each coherent block.

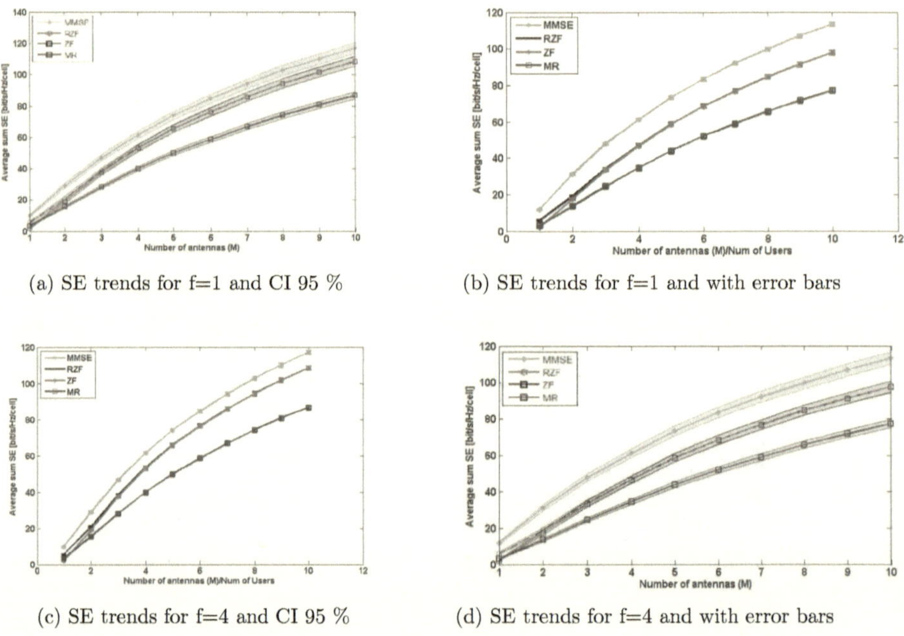

(a) SE trends for f=1 and CI 95 %   (b) SE trends for f=1 and with error bars

(c) SE trends for f=4 and CI 95 %   (d) SE trends for f=4 and with error bars

Figure 4.15: Effect of Pilot Reuse factors on Spectral Efficiency:Precoding Methods

4.3.3   Precoding Simulation : Experiment 3c

After simulation experiments were done for the uplink case, equivalent experiments were done for the downlink scenarios. The graphs in Figure 4.15 through 4.16 show the spectral efficiency trends for MMSE, RZF,ZF and MR precoding schemes. As in the receive combining scenarios, MMSE precoding performed better than the other three precoding schemes. RZF precoding was next followed by ZF. The least performing was MR precoding. The simulations were done for pilot reuse factors 1, 2, 4 and 8. In all cases the spectral efficiency trends improved with more antennas assumed. However it was noted that compared to the corresponding receive combining methods, precoding methods obtained inferior spectral efficiency values for all pilot reuse factors and for all values of assumed antenna elements. It also took comparatively more antenna elements for ZF performance to coincide with RZF for precoding signal processing.

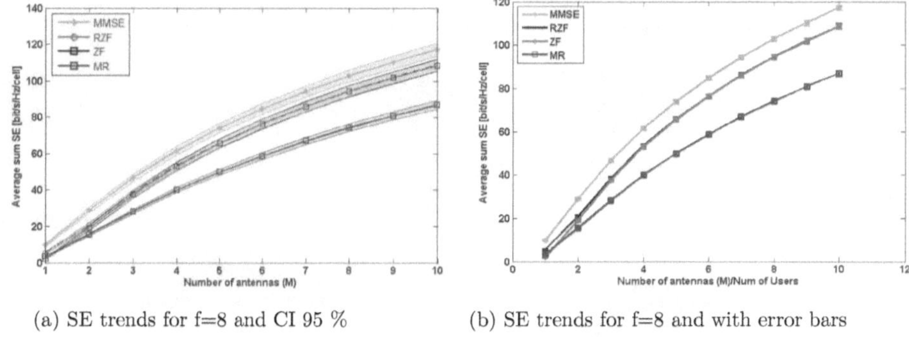

(a) SE trends for f=8 and CI 95 % (b) SE trends for f=8 and with error bars

Figure 4.16: Effect of Pilot Reuse factors on Spectral Efficiency:Precoding Methods

4.3.4 Precoding Simulation : Experiment 3d

As was done during receive combing experiments, the last experiment to investigate the effect of pilot reuse size on the spectral efficiency trends was done for the linear precoding methods under consideration. The trends are as shown in Figure 4.17. It appears the pilot reuse factor did not have much effect of the spectral efficiency trends for linear precoding methods.

4.4 Reflections on Experiments

Several experiment results were discussed at in this section. The first experiment looked at obtainable SEs in a single cell scenario for four receive combining methods. These are MMSE, RZF, ZF and MR receive combining methods. The second experiment set looked at a 16 cell scenario and varied the pilot reuse factor for the same receive combining methods. The maximum and minimum SE values for all the 16 cell grid signal processing simulation results are as shown in Table 4.4. It appears receive combining has higher corresponding SE values than the corresponding precoding methods. Receive combining seemed more sensitive to pilot reuse factor compared to precoding. The relationship between the maximum and minimum obtainable spectral efficiency with the pilot reuse factor was not very clear in these experiments.

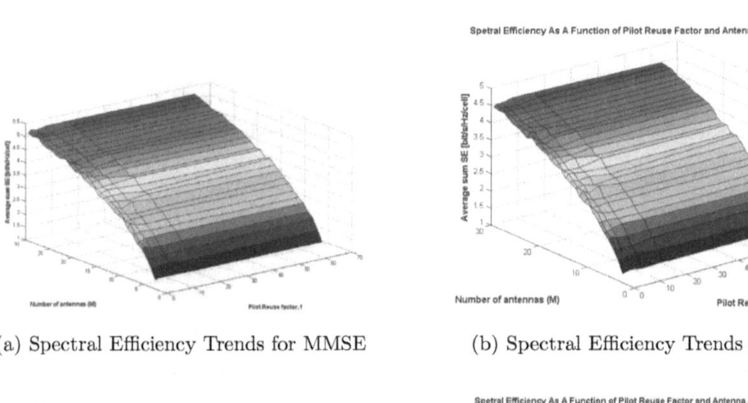

(a) Spectral Efficiency Trends for MMSE

(b) Spectral Efficiency Trends for RZF

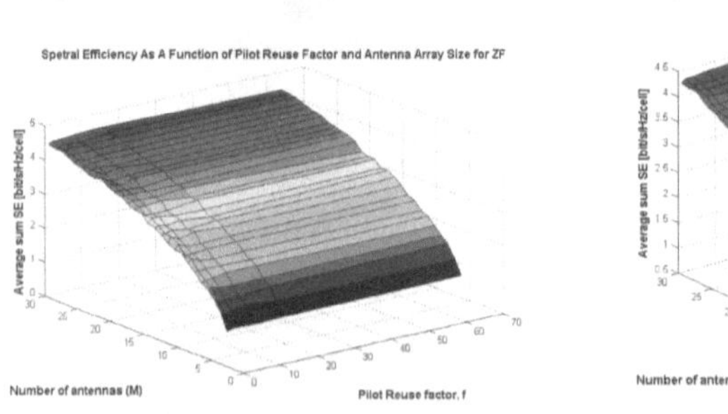

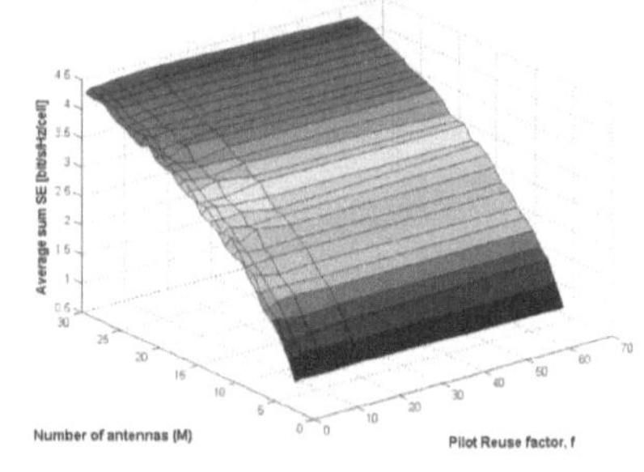

(c) Spectral Efficiency Trends for ZF

(d) Spectral Efficiency Trends for MR

Figure 4.17: Effect of Pilot Reuse factors on Spectral Efficiency:Precoding Methods

Table 4.4: Maximum Spectral Efficiencies for the 16 cell Network with 20 Users per cell

Signal Processing Method	Pilot Factor	Mimimum SE		Maximum SE	
		Precoding	Detection	Precoding	Detection
MMSE	1	10	31	30	95
RZF	1	10	21	29.5	79
ZF	1	7	5.8	29	79
MR	1	4.8	14	20.7	40
MMSE	2	10	30	30	98
RZF	2	10	20	29.5	75
ZF	2	7.4	5	29	75
MR	2	4.8	12	20.7	37
MMSE	4	10.4	23	30.4	85
RZF	4	10	15	29.4	58
ZF	4	7.4	4	29.2	58
MR	4	4.7	9	20.7	27

A third set of simulation experiments were done using the 64 cell grid scenario with various signal processing methods. Receive combining methods were looked at first, then the corresponding precoding methods were also evaluated. Table 4.5 shows the maximum and minimum spectral efficiency values obtained when the pilot reuse factor was varied. Again detection methods performed better than precoding methods. The last experiment varied the pilot size to 64 as was shown in Figure4.14 and Figure4.17. The results show that there is an optimal value of the pilot reuse factor that can be derived for simulating a given network.

Table 4.4 and Table 4.5 show the maximum and minimum spectral efficiency values obtained using the 16 cell grid and the 64 cell grid respectively. In all cases detection methods performed superior to their precoding counterparts. The relative trends between the signal processing methods, be it decoding (receive combining) or precoding were the same.

In modeling the cellular networks, the number of users in a cell, the assumed antenna elements and square shape of cells were arbitrarily chosen. It was necessary to chose figures such that the simulations could be completed in an ordinary computer. With a supercomputer, more users in cell could have been assumed. A regular shape for a cell helps make the work more reproducible. It was known that cells are normally sectorized in most real networks.

Table 4.5: Maximum Spectral Efficiencies for the 64 cell Network with 16 users per cell

Signal Processing Method	Pilot Factor	Mimimum SE		Maximum SE	
		Precoding	Detection	Precoding	Detection
MMSE	1	0.6	14.64	5.54	33.26
RZF	1	0.17	8.8	4.8	30.1
ZF	1	0.06	3.05	4.8	30.1
MR	1	0.06	9.33	4.8	20.68
MMSE	2	0.62	15.51	5.5	35.65
RZF	2	0.18	9.39	4.75	31.67
ZF	2	0.05	3.51	4.75	31.67
MR	2	0.05	9.39	2.77	20.52
MMSE	4	0.59	13.76	5.48	32.48
RZF	4	0.16	7.99	4.72	28.08
ZF	4	0.06	3.06	4.72	28.08
MR	4	0.06	7.99	2.75	17.54
MMSE	8	0.6	7.82	5.53	18.89
RZF	8	0.18	4.34	4.78	15.75
ZF	8	0.06	1.85	4.78	15.75
MR	8	0.06	4.34	2.77	9.57

4.5 Discussion of Results

The results obtained from this study show that the spectral efficiency of massive MIMO does increase with increase in antennas installed at the base station. This was consistently true regardless of which receive combining method was used in sections 4.1 through 4.3. For precoding signal processing the same effect on spectral efficiency was observed as presented in the same sections.

MMSE, RZF, ZF and MR were looked at in this study. The simulations done for an uncorrelated channel do motivate the case for many antenna elements at a massive MIMO base station. It was noted in the literature review earlier that non-linear receive combining methods are more expensive and computationally more complex to implement. However the non-linear signal processing methods are optimal. Linear signal processing receive combining methods like MMSE, RZF, ZF and MR are sub-optimal but computationally less complex. Maximum Likelihood (ML) detection is an example of a non-linear method that is optimal. Its computational complexity is $\mathcal{O}(M^N)$, where $M-$ary is the order of modulation while N is the number of transmit antennas [51] used. In comparison the computational complexity of ZF is roughly $\mathcal{O}(N^3)$ [51]. However the linear receive combining methods do perform differently among themselves. For this reason, the simulations done were for the performance of MMSE, ZF, RZF and MR which are all linear.

Assuming an uncorrelated fading channel in section 4.1.1, RZF and MMSE had more or less the same spectral efficiency values for the same of number of antenna elements assumed at the base station. For the lower number of antenna elements, spectral efficiency of ZF was about 50% that of MMSE. However as the ratio of antenna elements to users increased to 4 times, ZF spectral efficiency caught up with both MMSE and RZF receive combining methods. This confirms the literature [40] that says MMSE performance converges to ZF at high SNR.

For MR, when the number of antenna elements was equal to the number of users in a cell, the spectral efficiency of ZF was less than 25% of that for MMSE. However, as the number antenna elements were increased to 10 times the number of users, the spectral efficiency for MR increased towards the other signal processing methods, but at a much slower rate than that RZF and ZF.

The first simulation results in section 4.1.1 were for an uncorrelated channel. In reality wireless channels are likely to have some level of correlation. In order to model a more likely propagation channel, it was thus thought necessary to perform subsequent simulations using a Rayleigh correlated fading channel. In section 4.1.2, as was expected, the spectral efficiency performance for all signal processing methods was lower for the correlated channel compared to the uncorrelated channel case. RZF and MMSE showed the same trends as were observed for the uncorrelated channel case. In section 4.1.2, up to the point when number of antenna elements was twice the number of users, the spectral efficiency for MR was higher than that for ZF. After that particular point, ZF performance improved and approached both RZF and MMSE. By the point when the number of antenna elements to users ratio reached 10, the performance of ZF had caught up with RZF and MMSE. The situation was however different for MR. Its spectral efficiency performance as a function of the number of antenna elements was rather gradual.

The next simulations were performed using a 16 cell grid network in section 4.2. Receive combining and precoding linear signal processing methods were looked at in sections 4.2.1 and 4.2.2 respectively. From the spectral efficiency trends obtained, there seems to be a gradual decrease in spectral efficiency performance for RZF, ZF and MR as the pilot reuse factor is increased. This is however not the case for MMSE, whose maximum SE peaked at pilot reuse factor of 2. The Spectral efficiency value is a function of the gains made from more accurate channel estimation due to availability of more pilot sequences and the reduction in samples reserved to carry actual data when pilot samples are increased. The results in section 4.2 were therefore not conclusive as far as the optimal value of the pilot reuse factor is concerned.

In order to more fully evaluate the effect of pilot reuse factor of spectral efficiency performance, a 64 cell grid network was built in section 4.3. Increasing the pilot reuse factor has two effects as explained in [4]. The more pilots we have, the more accurate the channel estimates to be realized. This improves the SE performance of a given signal processing method. The second effect is to reduce the number of samples used to carry user data. This has the effect of decreasing the spectral efficiency of a given signal processing method. The results obtained for a 64 cell for receive combining method in section 4.3.1 show that the spectral efficiency initially improve when the pilot reuse factor is increased. The performance then decreases for higher values of pilot reuse factors. This was the trend for all receive combining methods. For precoding methods in section 4.3.2, the performance was not so responsive to the changes in the pilot reuse factor. It may be thus necessary to build a model that allows for larger pilot reuse factor arrays to be tested.

The simulations that were performed in this investigation assumed that a UE would be assigned to its nearest base station. In reality it is not always like that as obstacles that weaken the radio signal may exist between the UE and the nearest base station. Use of digital terrain map could help in simulating relative signal strength from the signal from each base station in the network and decide the base station from which the strongest signal is received. In addition, UE assignment to a base station is subject to admission control and congestion control policies of a given network. However in spite of the simplifying assumptions made in these simulations, the author believes that the results obtained from the simulations are general enough to make conclusions on the massive MIMO network behavior.

Chapter 5

Conclusion and future work

This research involved putting together a significant amount work pieces together. The first piece was to do a literature review of the current works and then identifying possible research gaps that needed further work. After identifying and selecting the area to be focused on, then aims and objectives of the research were brought about. It was then to be decided on the methodology that would be implemented to achieve the desired objectives. Without equipment for field trials, all possible evaluations were to be done in software. MATLAB was chosen owing to its wide use in the research community. The next step was to choose what performance metrics could be evaluated in order to evaluate the chosen aspects of massive MIMO. Three network models were designed. These were a single network model, a 16 cell network model and a 64 cell network model. These models had centrally positioned base stations and users would be deployed randomly into each cell. The designs obtained were then translated into MATLAB code scripts. These would get tested then run and results saved, analyzed and then finally reported. This work also managed to produce a conference paper in the International Conference on Information Management and Industrial Engineering to be help in Cape Town, 2019 [52].

The rest of this chapter firstly discusses the results presented in the previous chapter. It then draws the main conclusions before suggesting the future works for this research topic.

5.1 Conclusion

Massive MIMO has a lot of potential as far as increasing the spectral efficiency of the next generation wireless systems is concerned. The simulation results obtained from this study and subsequent discussion and analysis of the results show that linear signal processing methods like ZF can approach the optimal performance of signal processing methods like MMSE. The key lies in increasing the number of antenna elements to be much more than the number of users.

Results from experiments in this study showed that ZF and RZF performance do approach MMSE as the number of antenna elements is increased. Up to 200 BS antenna elements were simulated for 20 users in a cell. In all cases, ZF was generally the most responsive detection method when the number of antenna elements was progressively increased from 20 to 200. The difference in performance of all detection methods for the correlated and uncorrelated channels shows that the dominant propagation environment may determine the number of antenna elements that is appropriate to obtain a certain spectral efficiency performance. The first set of simulations were only for a single cell, which implies that pilot pollution was not taken into account.

In a multicell environment pilot pollution is a reality. For this reason, the values of spectral efficiency obtained for single cell based simulations may be much higher than those that are possible in a realistic multicell environment. With figures above 100 bits/s/Hz it seems the spectral efficiency for legacy networks like LTE which is 15 bits/s/Hz can be improved by employing massive MIMO. The fact that at 200 antenna elements, RZF and ZF had converged to MMSE performance means that linear detection methods asymptotically become optimal with an increase in antenna elements at the base station. MR receive combining method was the least responsive to the addition of antenna elements at the base station.

The second set of simulations were done for a 16 cell grid network with an average of 20 users per cell. The results obtained showed that MMSE receive combining performs best, followed by RZF, then ZF and lastly MR. As the number of antennas was increased, ZF performance would approach RZF. The trends observed for receive combining methods were similar to those obtained for precoding methods. However precoding methods had comparatively lower spectral efficiency values.

Increasing the pilot reuse factor affects the obtainable SE in two ways as explained in [4]. It increases the accuracy of the channel approximations and also lowers the number of samples available for the user data. For this reason the combined effect of increasing pilot reuse is not straight forward. The results obtained for a 64 cell grid network showed that the spectral efficiency will initially improve as the pilot reuse factor increased, peaking at some value before going into a decreasing trend. This was pronounced for all receive combining methods. The same experiments were also done for corresponding precoding schemes. The spectral efficiency did not seem to vary that much for precoding schemes. It may therefore be necessary to do simulations for more pilot reuse factors for precoding schemes before drawing conclusions.

In conclusion, this study gave some useful insights into the possible use of linear detection and precoding methods for massive MIMO. It showed that the bigger the antenna to user ratio becomes, the more linear detection methods approach optimal performance as far as spectral efficiency is concerned. The actual spectral efficiency obtained will depend on linear detection method used and the dominant propagation conditions encountered. The study also showed that an optimal pilot reuse factor for a given network can be obtained so as to maximize the spectral efficiency performance of signal processing methods in massive MIMO.

5.2 Future Work

This research gave valuable insights into the spectral efficiency performance of massive MIMO systems. The potential of linear signal processing for detection and precoding was evaluated. The effect of pilot pollution on the spectral efficiency was also evaluated. There is however some more issues that may be investigated so as to understand massive MIMO more fully.

The following is a list of proposed future work on this topic:

- It is recommended that more multiple cell simulations for precoding maybe done so as to see the effect of pilot reuse factor size on the spectral efficiency performance.

- MSSE estimation method was used. In future it is planned to investigate the effect of other estimation techniques.

- This study did not simulate the energy efficiency aspects of massive MIMO. In future it is recommended to do so.

- There are also new versions of planning tools like Atoll 3.3.2 and Planet 7 which can simulate massive MIMO and 3D beam forming. It is thus planned to do more simulations in a more complex and yet more realistic propagation environment.

- Simulations to compare with non-linear signal processing methods like Dirty Paper Coding (DPC) and Maximum Likelihood (ML) methods shall be done

- The BER (Bit Error Ratio) performance of the signal processing methods shall be done.

Working on massive MIMO performance provided the author a very comprehensive platform to understand some of the issues regarding the potential implementation of the technology. From the results obtained from this research, it is hoped that more research can be built upon this work and more issues on massive MIMO shall be studied.